D1394827

"A brilliant and highly readable account of why so many traditional Labour supporters backed Boris Johnson in 2019."

ROBERT PESTON, ITV POLITICAL EDITOR

"A meticulously researched, frank and thoughtful guide to the United Kingdom's new swing voters, what drives them and what that means for our politics."

STEPHEN BUSH, *NEW STATESMAN* POLITICAL EDITOR

"Politics is always personal. The conversations here bring to life the changing mood among the individuals who gradually lost faith in Labour and granted the Tories a thumping majority. The warning to all politicians – voters don't belong to you."

LAURA KUENSSBERG, BBC POLITICAL EDITOR

"While others theorise about why lifelong Labour voters in the Red Wall seats switched to the Tories in such vast numbers, Deborah Mattinson takes the radical approach of going to ask them. What they said is frank, forthright and fascinating. This calm, compelling account by someone who has seen Labour at its best and worst reveals the real people behind the polls. It will make for difficult reading for both parties, but after years of neglect they expect to be heard – and no party can expect to win without listening."

MATT CHORLEY, *THE TIMES*

"In this devastating new assessment of the fall of Labour's Red Wall, Deborah Mattinson unpicks our most recent history with deftness, clarity and piercing awareness. Matching engaging description with immense research and, above all, convincing argument, she finally gives voice to the 'long forgotten', definitively reporting how the Red Wall turned blue."

AYESHA HAZARIKA, *EVENING STANDARD*

"Deborah Mattinson brilliantly deconstructs the Red Wall, brick by brick, using her own research and expertise, helping us to understand this overlooked group and what makes it tick. For our leaders, learning the lessons of *Beyond the Red Wall* will be key to whoever wins the next general election."

CHRISTOPHER HOPE, *DAILY TELEGRAPH*

"Deborah Mattinson has long been a shrewd and sympathetic analyst of voters and their motivations. Rich with real voices, *Beyond the Red Wall* is a must-read for anyone who wants to understand what drove so many in Labour's heartlands to desert the party in 2019 – and what it might take to win them back."

HEATHER STEWART, *THE GUARDIAN* POLITICAL EDITOR

DEBORAH MATTINSON

BEYOND THE RED WALL

WHY LABOUR LOST, HOW THE CONSERVATIVES WON AND WHAT WILL HAPPEN NEXT?

Biteback Publishing

First published in Great Britain in 2020 by
Biteback Publishing Ltd, London
Copyright © Deborah Mattinson 2020

ISBN 978-1-78590-604-6

10 9 8 7 6 5 4 3 2 1

A CIP catalogue record for this book is available from the British Library.

Set in Minion Pro and Trade Gothic

Printed and bound in Great Britain by
CPI Group (UK) Ltd, Croydon CR0 4YY

MIX
Paper from
responsible sources
FSC® C020471

*For Clara, Theo and Francis, whose idea this was,
and for Dave, with much love and thanks.*

CONTENTS

PART ONE

THE RED WALL AND ITS PEOPLE

1

INTRODUCTION: WHAT REALLY HAPPENED IN DECEMBER 2019?

'They forgot about people like us, up here. We're the forgotten people. I'd like to think that might change now. I'd like a party just for once to say, yeah, we've heard what you're saying, we're going to do this.'

Ian, from Accrington, described himself as a 'plumber-slash-handyman'. Well informed and articulate, he spoke for all the other men sitting round the table one blustery evening in February 2020. His frustration with politics was palpable. I was to hear the same feelings expressed again and again in the coming weeks: exasperation, even anger, with politicians who no longer understood or supported people like Ian. Ian, like pretty much everyone I spoke to, also described himself as a lifelong Labour voter. Ian, like pretty much everyone I spoke to, had voted Conservative for the first time in December 2019.

Former Tory strategist James Kanagasooriam is widely

credited with inventing the concept of the Red Wall. As a child, he had been given a duvet cover featuring an Ordnance Survey map of the UK as a birthday present. He spent many evenings memorising the strange-sounding names of towns he had never visited and probably never would. As a teenager, starting to study politics, he was intrigued to see that, when the political map of Britain was overlaid on the duvet map, the bottom half was blue while the top half was red. He later described the sixty-odd seats forming the boundary between red and blue as a wall partly because of their geographical positioning: they form a physical barrier, a curved spine that rises up through the centre of the country, starting in the Midlands, reaching up to the north then across into North Wales, carving the country in two. He noted, however, that the wall was much more than that. It was an ideological divide.

I first came across the term just a few months before the 2019 election. The *Times* columnist Rachel Sylvester told me she had been talking to her Tory contacts, who had confided that they were targeting a group of long-standing Labour seats that they thought might just be winnable. She explained which seats they were: 'They're calling them the Red Wall.' I was sceptical: these were seats that had rejected the Tories for decades – in some cases for ever. They had stayed Labour because being Labour was part of their identity, practically written into their DNA. Voting Tory would surely be anathema to them. I struggled to imagine these loyal Labour working-class communities ever being able to stomach switching to the Conservatives, especially now, when the party was led by a Latin-spouting

Old Etonian. It wasn't called the Red Wall for nothing. Yet, on 12 December, starting with Blyth Valley, I watched as seat after Labour seat collapsed to the Tories, challenging all conventional wisdoms about political tribalism. The Red Wall had turned blue.

Listening to voters the following week, 'surprised', 'relieved' and 'hopeful' were the words they used most often to describe their feeling about the election result. This response was as likely to come from former Labour voters as long-standing Conservatives. Even some Labour voters claimed to be relieved. The shock result had confounded their concern that the election would not be decisive. Continuing the stasis that had paralysed the nation for the previous four years was the outcome they had most feared. 'If there's a hung parliament again, we'll have to have a penalty shoot-out to sort it out,' Mike, an undecided voter from Birmingham, had suggested a couple of weeks before polling day. Others in the focus group laughed, but Mike stood by his idea, pointing out that we were happy enough to settle a rather more important contest – the World Cup – in this way, so, why on earth not an election?

It's striking that voters had spent so much time worrying about the possibility of a hung parliament, given the decisiveness of the eventual result. The Tories won 43.6 per cent of the vote and 365 seats. Labour's vote dropped to 32.2 per cent and just 203 seats. It was their biggest defeat since 1935. I usually pride myself on my performance on the office sweepstake at BritainThinks, the insight and strategy consultancy I co-founded ten years ago. This time I was bang on with the Tory vote share – up a relatively modest 1.2 per cent from 2017. However, I let myself down badly by underestimating the sheer scale of Labour's loss – down 7.8 per cent from last time, leaving the party largely confined to big cities and a handful of university towns. The Tories had surpassed their own most optimistic predictions, taking an eighty-seat lead. Labour will now need 124 net gains to achieve a majority of just one. It's quite a challenge.

Of course, the biggest upset on what was generally a miserable night for Labour turned out to be just how many of the Tories' wins came from the Red Wall. These old coal, steel and manufacturing constituencies were regarded as the home of the traditional Labour vote: working-class men and women whose loyalty had underpinned past Labour victories, including the 1997 landslide. Labour owned these places – many voters had never voted anything else – but all that had changed. Post-election analysis suggested that long-standing class-based loyalties mattered much less now. In fact, the Tories led across all social classes in 2019, performing especially strongly with C2DE social groups (semi-skilled and unskilled workers: drivers, retail workers, care assistants; people who might self-define as 'working class'). They also won nearly half of all manual workers and 58 per cent of those whose educational attainment was GCSE level or less.

In contrast, Labour did particularly well with the most highly qualified voters, winning 43 per cent of graduates, of whom just 29 per cent voted Conservative. Age correlates closely with qualifications, and the new battle lines now seem to be more about age than class. The younger you are, the more likely you are to have benefited from higher education. The Tories won resoundingly with older voters, enjoying a 47-point lead amongst the over 65s, while Labour achieved a 43-point lead with 18–24s. This much, though, could be regarded as business as usual, the general pattern of the past few elections. The biggest change turned out to be amongst middle-aged voters: we saw a swing of seven points from Labour to Tory amongst 35–54-year-olds. In 2019, thirty-nine became the age at which you would be more likely to vote Tory. Just two years earlier, in 2017, it had been forty-seven.

Age had been important in the 2016 referendum too. Leave voters were typically older and less well educated, Remain voters the opposite. Crucially, the 2016 vote also pinpoints a values divide, neatly illustrated by Lord Ashcroft's post-referendum polling. He asked voters whether they believed that a set of concepts including multiculturalism, feminism and social liberalism were a 'force for good' or a 'force for ill'. The strong and emotive language used in the question's wording might have been rejected in a dive to the middle ground – but it wasn't. The findings demonstrated the polarised nature of the population. Eight out of ten people who said these 'isms' were a 'force for ill' were Leave voters; seven out of ten who said they were a 'force for good' were Remainers.

My focus groups at the time illustrated the depth of this divide. I was taken aback by the degree of contempt that each group showed for one another's opinions. Leavers thought Remainers were 'out of touch', 'politically correct', 'superior' and 'stuck up'. Leavers were angry and resentful and felt that they were being looked down on. They were not wrong. Remainers described Leavers as 'misguided' at best and would often go to some lengths to explain how easily they had been hoodwinked. This would always imply, even if not overtly stated – and it often was – that Leavers were 'ignorant' or 'stupid'. Sometimes Remainers would go further and condemn Leavers as 'racist'. Red Wall constituencies were very much more likely to have voted Leave rather than Remain: some had Leave winning more than 70 per cent of the vote. As James Kanagasooriam had noticed, that wall really was much more than a physical divide: it was, he told me, about 'attitudes towards culture, state, belonging and place'. It had become what Arlie Russell Hochschild describes as an 'empathy wall' in her brilliant book about the American right, *Strangers in Their Own Land*: 'A wall that is an obstacle to deep understanding of another person, one that can make us feel indifferent or even hostile to those who hold different beliefs.'

Listening to voters over three decades has taught me that Brexit was a symptom, not a cause: exposure of these stark cultural and ideological differences had been a very long time coming. In 2010, I wrote my first book, the story of the birth – and death – of New Labour, told through the eyes of the voter. I called it *Talking to a Brick Wall* because I believed that Labour in government had gradually lost the knack of listening to voters, a quality that had delivered its richly deserved electoral victory in 1997. On reflection, I believe everyone who held a senior position in Labour between then and now deserves some share of the blame for what happened on 12 December 2019. Here's my confession: other than the occasional by-election, at no point in the decades that I spent advising Labour did we ever consider running focus groups or polling in any of the Red Wall seats. Their reliability was seen as a given – quite frankly, they were taken for granted. This was not just Labour's oversight, though. These voters were neglected by the entire political class. Labour felt that they didn't need to worry about their 'heartland constituencies', populated by voters who would never let them down, who would always be on side. The Conservatives ignored them for a different reason: they were deemed totally unwinnable, so there was really no point.

All that changed in 2019. In the aftermath of the political upheaval of Brexit, the Conservatives turned their sights to the Red Wall, gambling that, maybe this time, their fortunes would change. Meanwhile, Labour compounded the errors of a very poorly run campaign by redeploying local activists away from defending Red Wall constituencies and sending them instead to seats considered winnable targets or strategically important, like Uxbridge, Boris Johnson's own seat. On the day, Johnson increased his majority, winning 52.6 per cent of the vote, and Labour made just one gain in the entire country: Putney. Of the sixty seats that Labour lost, more than two-thirds were in the Red Wall. The next day, a gleeful newly elected Tory Prime Minister rubbed salt into Labour's wound by running his victory rally in Sedgefield, previously the seat of one well-known Red Wall Labour MP, Tony Blair, Labour's most electorally successful leader ever.

In this book, I have set out to understand who the 'Red Wallers' are, what matters to them, why they abandoned Labour, why they voted Conservative and what will win their votes in the next election. As well as drawing on BritainThinks' own research and many published data sources, I chose three constituencies from different parts of the Red Wall to conduct 'deep dives' into voters' views: Hyndburn in Lancashire, Darlington up in the north-east and Stoke-on-Trent in the Midlands.

It's important to be clear that I was not looking to meet a cross-section of voter opinion in each constituency. This is *qualitative* research, small-scale and in-depth, and my aim was to dig beneath the polling to really understand the motivations of people who had voted Labour consistently in the past but had chosen to vote Conservative – often for the first time – in 2019. My recruitment method was typical for this kind of research, used by market research agencies up and down the country for a multitude of commercial and social research projects, testing advertising and PR messages, exploring new product development and, of course, looking at how voters decide which way to vote. I thought through, as precisely as I could, exactly who I wanted to speak to and developed a short recruitment specification. In this instance, the brief was simple: I was looking for men and women drawn from the C2DE social grades that dominate many Red Wall constituencies, typically manual workers, carers, drivers, construction workers and factory workers. I wanted a spread of ages from late thirties up to mid-seventies. In terms of race, people were recruited to reflect the area.

The only other crucial criteria for the interviewees' profiles was their past voting behaviour: I asked for everyone to be past Labour voters who had switched to the Conservatives at the 2019 election. This qualifying question was buried in a recruitment questionnaire covering a wide range of different attitudinal questions, as, ideally, I wanted to avoid people coming along with prior knowledge of what they were going to be talking about, making it possible to gauge spontaneous views and avoid over-thinking. I also try to avoid people who are unusually interested in the subject under discussion. This spec was then shared with my network of professional recruiters, identifying those working in the right locations. These recruiters used a combination of street and database recruitment to find people who most precisely fit the bill. The final stage was a screening interview to ensure that the potential interviewees were who they said they were. We typically pay a cash incentive for people to attend – at £50 or so for ninety minutes, there is a risk that some may be tempted to blag their way into the session despite their ineligibility to attend, and we try to prevent this with a quick call to verify the information provided. Of course, we were looking for ordinary people, not professional focus groupies.

In *Talking to a Brick Wall*, I included a chapter entitled, 'What Is a Focus Group?' In it I recounted the history of focus groups, particularly their use in politics. I also talked through some of the techniques that are typically used in such groups, and why; the importance of skilled moderation and what that looks like; the use of 'projective techniques' and a few examples, e.g. 'Think about a friend who voted X and tell me why you think they did' – or the ever popular 'If X leader was an animal / car / drink, what would they be and why?'

After their first use in the UK by Mrs Thatcher and her team, focus groups went through a resurgence of popularity, as used by New Labour, and then a period in which the very expression provoked derision. Now, in the Boris Johnson era, they are back at the heart of political strategy-setting, championed by Dominic Cummings, Johnson's chief advisor. My own respect for focus groups and what we can learn from them has been constant throughout this period. I always use them alongside other methods, including large-scale polling, deliberative research like citizens' juries and observational ethnographic techniques. For this book, as well as using focus groups I have looked at all the relevant available published data sources, conducted long, in-home ethnographic interviews and simply wandered round the streets in the three constituencies I have focused on, chatting to people and watching them go about their daily lives. In each place I conducted focus groups with long-standing Labour voters who had switched to Tory, as well as extended interviews, spending time with people in their homes, listening to them talking about their day: doing shopping, going to work, walking the dog or picking up their kids or grandkids from school. I also interviewed the out-going Labour MP and the incoming Tory MP in each location.

The places I visited are all very different, but they share many common characteristics. The people there all believe, to varying degrees, that they have been neglected and overlooked by power brokers in the south. London feels a long way away. They rejoice in an illustrious industrial past and each place is incredibly proud of its own distinctive identity. However, the future looks much less promising and they are worried for their kids and grandkids. The people I met are proud too: proud of being working class, proud of their local communities and even prouder of the country, although recent years brought changes that some were wary of. They tend to be sceptical of politics and politicians, both local and national. The failure – until very recently – of the Brexit process has enhanced this feeling, however they voted in the 2016 referendum. Their long-standing Labour vote had seemed a natural choice, but Labour was different now. As respected psephologist Paula Surridge put it: 'Labour had been moving away from working-class voters for some time, but when Corbyn took over this became turbo-charged.' Their Tory vote, often offered hesitantly, was now something with which they have grown more comfortable. Boris Johnson, despite being 'posh', seemed, in December 2019, to 'get' them. Now they were full of hope.

Voters reward most new governments with a honeymoon period, but it never lasts as long as the government might hope, and those who have tried something new can be swift to question their choice. This crunch point might come about as a result of something driven by the government itself (for example, the new government's first Budget), or it may have been created by a change of key personnel: the debut of a new opposition leader, for instance. Sometimes, the moment could be triggered by external events. Very few of us, however, would have predicted that this government's honeymoon period would be abruptly ended by the arrival of a massive, unprecedented global catastrophe in the shape of the coronavirus pandemic. As my visits to Red Wall towns got underway, the crisis began to take a grip on the nation, transforming the lives of ordinary British people everywhere. My visit to Hyndburn took place almost a month before it all kicked off, but I was in Darlington at the beginning of a week that was to see the closure of theatres, cinemas, restaurants and pubs. Stoke-on-Trent, the final visit in my schedule, was forced to become virtual interviews and focus groups, conducted online as lockdown made face-to-face meetings impossible. Boris Johnson ended up being tested much earlier in his premiership, and, given his own battle with the virus, tested in a much more personal way, than he might have expected. In a fast-changing world where attitudes fluctuated daily, it was an increasingly daunting challenge to keep abreast of the impact of this seismic shift.

As I write, the crisis is still unfolding, but, in my penultimate chapter, I have tried to assess the likely effect of the pandemic on voters' views across the country, and on Red Wallers specifically. How will they judge this government and how may it change who becomes the next? At first sight, as our anxious nation looked for leadership, the government's reputation fared well, with ratings improving enough to be net positive for the first time in more than a decade. It looked good too for Boris Johnson, whose personal ratings soared. However, comparing the coronavirus crisis with the closest parallel in recent history, the financial crisis of 2008, offers some stark lessons. Although the then Prime Minister, Gordon Brown, gained an early poll boost and widespread approval for his handling of the crisis, this failed to translate into any long-term advantage. Worse still, as the Tories' messaging hit home to devastating effect, Labour saw all its careful work to boost its reputation for economic competency unravel. At the 2010 election, voters found it easy to believe an attack about Labour's economic strategy because it spoke to long-held views about the party's lack of fiscal discipline. This is a spectre that haunts Labour still, more than ten years later.

Discussing politics, the pandemic and their impact on people's lives, everyone I have spoken to over the past few months has been honest, sometimes devastatingly so, and incredibly generous with their time at a very difficult period, characterised by uncertainty, frustration and fear. Voters in the Red Wall constituencies deserve a better deal and I hope that, whatever happens politically, they get it.

2

THE RED WALL: WHAT IS IT? WHERE IS IT? WHO LIVES THERE?

'You could draw a line right across the middle of Britain – the bottom half is the have's and the top half is the have not's.'

Although the term is now well known, at least in Westminster circles, there is no universal definition of which seats make up the Red Wall. James Kanagasooriam, the Tory strategist credited with inventing the concept, talks about a wall stretching up from the Midlands to North Wales then across to Merseyside. He excluded the north-east, whose ex-mining constituencies he categorises separately (although, prior to the 2019 election, he also correctly identified these as fruitful Tory targets). For the purposes of this book I have included the north-east in my definition of Red Wall seats that Labour lost to the Tories in 2019 and carried out fieldwork in Darlington as well as Stoke and Hyndburn. I kept in touch with the people I met and spoke to them again at various points to get an update on their views as events occurred: the 2020 Budget, the election of Keir Starmer as Labour leader and, of course, coronavirus.

Since the drama of 12 December 2019, there has been a lot of talk about the Red Wall, with many assumptions made about the people who live in these constituencies by politicians and commentators who are unlikely ever to meet any of them. In fact, the Red Wall is home to some 4.7 million people who collectively represent approximately 8 per cent of the population of England and Wales. Very few of the people that I spoke to had heard of the term 'Red Wall', none used it themselves and, on being told about it, many were bemused. This is partly because none sees themselves as part of any group, particularly a group defined by voting patterns – although, as we shall see, a sense of belonging is something the Labour Party has relied heavily upon in the past. My focus is on people who abandoned Labour in 2019. These are the people that the Tories now have to hold on to, and that Labour must win back to be in with a shout of winning again. Those I heard from could not be seen as a homogenous group, and have as many characteristics that pull them apart as those that draw them together. However, while clear differences emerge by geography, demography and attitudes, there are significant economic and sociological similarities and patterns, and themes consistently emerge reflecting how Red Wallers feel about their lives, about where they live and about the country as a whole.

The first of these is precisely why they would never identify as a group with 'other Red Wallers'. Many share a striking feeling of isolation: the sense of being physically separate from the rest of the country. Two-thirds of Red Wallers live in towns, while just 15 per cent live in cities (only 3 per cent in major cities) and 17 per cent in villages. Many of these towns, like Accrington in Hyndburn, are small settlements near to large conurbations that are geographically close but not easily accessible by public transport, with major implications for how people live and work. Stoke-on-Trent Central, apparently a city, is in fact a collection of six towns strung together, each with their own identities and little sense of collective spirit. Many of the people I met lived their lives almost entirely within a few miles of their home and felt constrained by this. This turned out to be particularly true of the women I met, who often felt trapped by their domestic responsibilities.

Michelle, who runs a 'butty shop' in Accrington – a small café selling pies, sandwiches and hot and cold drinks to local workers – lives above the shop and told me that her social life extended only as far as a street two blocks away. She explained that she never went 'into town' – the town centre was just a few hundred yards away at the end of her road; I'd walked from there to her home in less than five minutes. The Resolution Foundation's analysis of ONS data in their 'Painting the Towns Blue' study confirms that Red Wall voters spend less time commuting than people from any other part of the country – typically just twenty-four minutes from home to work – and that they are much more likely to drive. Most of the people I met drove absolutely everywhere: to shop, to work, to socialise. When I asked focus group participants to identify what they liked least about living where they do, poor transport connections was one of the most frequent mentions, especially from male voters, who are more likely to be working further from home but often find the journey challenging. Cheaper or free parking was frequently at or near the top of people's wish-lists, as was cheaper fuel. Both make a dramatic difference to weekly budgeting for those dependent on driving.

For most Red Wallers, this isolation is not just about being physically separate. They feel 'apart' from the rest of the country in other ways too. This was often articulated using the term 'left behind', which, coincidentally, is probably the expression most often used about them by commentators and politicians. The north–south divide, which was referred to again and again, is an economic as well as a geographical division. I heard the term 'southerners' repeatedly used disparagingly, but the frustration is less about how Red Wallers see the south and more about how they believe they are seen by the rest of the country: overlooked, sneered at and looked down upon. This fuels the most powerful sentiment that I heard everywhere I went: a deep feeling of loss, specifically a strong belief that the place they call home had once been considered important to the country as a whole but is now ignored, seen as inconsequential and, as a result, has been allowed to decay.

Many of the people that I spoke to told me the stories of their town's former glory with the greatest of pride. Some had parents and grandparents who had worked in the local mill, in the brick works, in the potteries or, like my own grandfather in Darlington, where I was born, on the railways. There was understandable eagerness to share stories about the contribution their families had made and the place in history their home had earned. Many Red Wall towns have strong links with the armed forces too, and this was frequently mentioned. In Accrington, several people talked about the 'Accrington Pals', a local battalion of Kitchener's army in the First World War: 'The Accrington Pals paid a terrible price – almost every young man round here signed up. Almost none came home. My great-grandad was lucky,' said one, talking about the First World War heroes widely celebrated in the town. Others had just grown-up absorbing the glory of their area's heritage. And should they ever forget, there is physical evidence everywhere you look: the majestic mills in Accrington, the railway station in Darlington, the beautiful bottle kilns in Stoke-on-Trent are there to remind them.

The three locations I chose to visit did indeed all have the proudest of histories: Accrington had once been at the heart of the textile industry and was also famous for NORI bricks (iron backwards, so-called because of its extraordinary strength). The NORI brick, historically made at the Accrington brickworks, was used to build the Blackpool Tower, Battersea Power Station and, at the very peak of its glory, the Empire State Building. Darlington, of course, was the birthplace of the world's first passenger-bearing steam train, Locomotion No. 1, built in the 1820s by George Stephenson. Meanwhile, Stoke-on-Trent was home to the potteries since the seventeenth century, with companies like Royal Doulton, Wedgwood, Minton and Spode established and based there, exporting their beautiful wares around the world.

But that golden era is now firmly in the past. Accy's brick-works have had a chequered recent history, opening, closing down, being reopened (most recently with some fanfare by David Cameron and George Osborne in 2015) and then again in jeopardy, now employing tens rather than hundreds or thousands of people. Darlington railworks closed down in 1962, and now Locomotion No. 1 is at risk of being moved away from its current home, the Head of Steam museum. Stoke's station entrance is famous too, boasting a statue of Josiah Wedgwood, founder of the china company that still bears his name. However, many of the potteries have now closed and Stoke's most well-known entrepreneur today has a very different claim to fame: Peter Coates, founder of the global online-betting leader, bet365. The Coates family are now billionaires, and the firm sponsors the beloved Stoke City football team. The company is thought to be a good employer but now employs fewer than 4,000 people, while in its heyday ten times that worked for the potteries and related industries.

This sense of loss inevitably translates into another recurring theme: the profound lack of opportunity, especially for young people, many of whom struggle to find education, training or employment in the area of their hometown. I heard from parents who were trying, reluctantly, to persuade their children to move away from home. In Accrington, with its long-held and proud connection with the army, several dads told me that this was what they hoped their sons might do: 'He's a good lad, hard-working, but there's nothing for him here. The army would set up him. Give him a good start.' Yet the Resolution

Foundation's study of Red Wall seats, suggests that these dads' efforts might be in vain: while few young people are moving into the area, even fewer are leaving – despite deep-rooted concerns about how little the area has to offer. Instead, if you are young and living in the Red Wall, you are much less likely than young people living in other areas to move away. Most of the people I met talked about their nearby cities (Manchester, Birmingham, Newcastle) as if they were another country. Many had never visited London, and abroad was discussed as somewhere for an occasional holiday in the sun, rarely as somewhere that might offer career opportunities.

I met Kayla, a 32-year-old catering worker in Accrington, who told me how she would actually quite like to live 'down south', possibly in Swindon, where she had family whom she occasionally visited. She believed that she and, eventually, her older children may have been able to get better training and better jobs in the south, but was concerned that the cost of living would be prohibitive – in particular the likely cost of housing was going to make it very hard to move. Privately rented properties are significantly cheaper in Red Wall constituencies than in the country as a whole. The Red Wall has also experienced lower house-price increases. The cab driver who picked me up from the station when I arrived in Hyndburn made this point well. When I asked him what he liked about living locally he didn't hesitate for a moment: 'Cheap flats!' Checking on Rightmove later, I discovered that a decent-looking two-bed flat would set you back just £32,000, while a three-bed house with garage and garden was yours for around £120,000. Darlington was a little more expensive, maybe £140,000 for a three-bed house, and Stoke was in between. The cheapest property that I found was a three-bed fixer-upper in Accrington for £29,950. You wouldn't get much for that 'down south'.

As well as worries about young people's future careers, there was a common perception that the area did not provide enough for them to do. Everywhere I went I heard about youth clubs closing down and playing fields falling into disrepair or being built on. Asked what he would do if he could change one thing, Gordon, a retired electrician in Accrington, told me he'd build a youth club with good sporting facilities. He was worried about how little there was for the 'young uns' to do. Colin, a self-employed 'brickie' from Stoke-on-Trent, also put 'better sports and recreation facilities for kids' at the top of his wish-list for his local area. Those with teenaged children or grandchildren were not just worried for their own kids but for the impact on the neighbourhood. Some talked about the knock-on impact on low-level crime and anti-social behaviour. Ali, who works in a customer services call centre as well as caring for her grandchildren, felt intimidated by the numbers of young people simply hanging around on street corners or in the 'dead' town centre. Maureen, mother of three 'boys' (aged thirty-nine, forty-three and forty-seven), works in Debenhams in Darlington and told me she now feels nervous about going out at night: 'It's the abusive youth, shouting their mouths off, swearing and climbing on the bus shelter at the end of my road.'

The Resolution Foundation analysis also shows that Red Wall constituencies have slower population growth than other areas in the UK, with fewer people moving in as a result of either internal or international migration. They have a smaller non-UK-born population than other areas, too. Anecdotally, these groups are also often less well integrated than they are in other regions. 'They keep themselves to themselves' was a grumble I heard frequently. This 'otherness' sometimes means that those groups become an easy target for those seeking to apportion blame for their own misfortune. For example, I regularly heard complaints about workers from other countries taking jobs away from locals either by undercutting their wages or through employers' political correctness. Julie, a part-time cleaner in Darlington, was furious that her son, 'a bright lad', had tried and failed twice to get into the police. 'They more or less said to him, "You're not the criteria,"' she told me. 'It annoys me that he missed out on the opportunity just because he wasn't a person of colour.' In Accrington, there is a significant Asian population, and I heard a few gripes about the council setting different rules for traders of Asian origin than those set for 'local' people: 'They're afraid they'll play the race card,' I was told. Michelle was convinced that her business had suffered as a result of unfair treatment. Julie used the 'race card' language too, saying she felt 'like a second-class citizen in my own country these days', adding, 'I'm not racist, I judge people for what they are, but it seems that we work hard and pay our taxes and immigrants get handouts and benefits that we're not able to get.' In Stoke, my focus groups, like Gareth Snell, the constituency's former MP, were insistent that different ethnic groups rubbed along fine. But when I asked a focus group of men what had changed for the worse locally, several mentioned the fast-growing Pakistani and Indian communities, seeing it as another symptom of the decline: 'They come here because it's cheap.'

Many Red Wallers shared strong feelings of resentment towards those they see as undeserving. Women were often more likely than their male counterparts to talk about the grievance they felt towards people they believed were 'milking the system' without ever having any intention of paying back. 'People should be made to work,' Tracey told me. As a carer she seemed to be permanently on duty, even taking a call from one of her charges during our session. 'It never stops,' she complained, adding, 'He's panicking a bit about something and it's only me that can calm him down.' The Resolution Foundation's analysis shows that the Red Wall has a higher rate of benefit spending per head than other areas. Much of this is in-work support that many female Red Wallers would be in receipt of – and, as it has fallen, they will be feeling the pinch even more, a factor that will be exaggerated as universal credit kicks in.

Most people I spoke to worked very hard indeed, but life seemed particularly tough for many of the women, often working multiple jobs – long hours for low pay. Penny, a care worker and foster parent, typically worked a six-day week and was still struggling to make ends meet. She talked about the high levels of stress caused by such intense working patterns, and its impact on her mental health. Penny was typical of the women I chatted with: often combining several part-time jobs and shouldering all the family's caring responsibilities, looking after children, grandchildren and sometimes elderly parents too. Money was tight and there was very little down time. Unsurprisingly, given the gender pay gap and greater likelihood to take responsibility for caring duties at home, these women felt their lives were harder than those of their men, though they dealt with this with affection rather than anger, mocking the men's incompetence. 'All men are completely rubbish!' joked one. Another had split up with her partner but ended up looking after his kids as well as her own: 'They preferred being with me,' she explained. Her ex now lived with his mum, who 'runs around after him – treats him like a kid'.

Some of these disparities in pay and the allocation of caring responsibilities are not unique to constituencies along the Red Wall. However, the problem seems to be more acute there. The Resolution Foundation's Blue Wall report highlights some important employment trends that were reflected many times in the conversations I had with Red Wallers. The Red Wall offers far fewer 'high-value' employment opportunities, being over-represented in retail and manufacturing – both declining sectors in the UK. It also over-indexes on healthcare employment. In reality, this probably means many low-paid caring jobs, the kind from which many of the women I listened to were struggling to make a living. The Red Wall under-indexes in the high-growth, high-value sectors: communications, finance, property, professional services and science, explaining why pay has fallen faster there than in other parts of the north, the Midlands and Wales. This was felt powerfully in Hyndburn and Stoke, while Darlington felt a little more positive. Mick, a Darlington-based kitchen-fitter, told me that, although the manufacturing all went more than twenty years ago, 'we've now got a stronger service sector here, with new jobs coming from Amazon, EE and some of the banks, so we're lucky'.

Yet despite Mick's optimism, a recurring Red Wall theme was the belief that its people have been not just neglected, but actually robbed. Many feel that the decline they observe in their place – and its impact on their lives and the lives of their families – is more sinister than just being 'left behind'. When some talked about the north–south divide, they talked as though they were witnessing a theft: they were not being deprived of funds but funds were being taken away from them and transferred to wealthier parts of the country, places where the political sun had been shining – London came in for special mention again and again. The resentment cut deep. Ian, a plumber and handyman in Accrington, described it like this: 'The north-west generates money and it all goes down to London. We create it, we need it, but they get it.' Top of mind here is infrastructure investment (in fairness, it's hard to im-agine living twenty miles outside of London and having to endure a one-hour, twenty-minute train commute, as Accring-ton commuters to Manchester would), but people also talk about the demise of the high street and, as discussed above, lack of high-value, high-paid jobs.

Unsurprisingly perhaps, all this has led to deep resentment. The resentment is born out of a perfect storm stoked by Red Wallers' feeling that their own hard work is unrewarded, the tangible evidence of lack of local investment, and the sense that other places are thriving at their expense. I asked one of the Stoke focus groups where they did their Christmas shopping. Never in Stoke, it turned out. Maybe they'd hop on a train to Manchester, the women told me. How about London, I asked, would they ever go to London to shop? 'No!' they said, half serious, half in jest. 'They're not getting my hard-earned cash down there!' In March 2020, BritainThinks ran a citizens' jury for the think tank Labour Together, an organisation seeking to unite the warring Labour Party factions. The jury formed part of a review commissioned to understand what went wrong in December 2019, which would be published the following June. Asked to create the 'ideal' political party, a team drawn from Red Wall constituencies brainstormed with enthusiasm. They summed up their thinking with the slogan 'Let's Make Britain Great Again'. The knowing nod to Trump led to a spontaneous chant of 'Let's build a wall,' which everyone joined with joking and laughing. 'Where would the wall be?' I asked, wondering if they were referring to the Red Wall, but I was quickly corrected. 'No! We'll build a wall around London!' shouted one and everyone cheered. They could not have been clearer: keeping Londoners in their place would be a very desirable outcome indeed.

Lancashire's position within England.

Hyndburn's position within Lancashire.

3

HYNDBURN

'My friend from Manchester came to stay. She said,
"It's like going back in time here."'

Storm Dennis arrived in Accrington the same day as I did. A misty veil of rain cloaked the town and a bitingly cold wind rattled the To Let signs along Stanley Street. I had left my umbrella in the hotel, so it was a relief to finally see Michelle's cafe. 'Butties, pies and cakes' promised the sign on the plastic awning that creaked and shook precariously in the gale. A welcoming haven to me and to the handful of local construction workers who dropped by for a filled bap or a meat and potato pie with gravy. Michelle, a smiley 56-year-old, greeted me warmly: 'Come in the back. Can I get you a brew?'

Michelle had moved to Accrington nearly fifteen years ago. A friend had moved there and, when visiting her, Michelle had been astonished by the property prices. She found she could buy her shop and the comfortable flat above for much less than the flat she owned thirty miles away in Cheshire. The move worked well, and she had soon met a new partner, grown very attached to his small son and started to make friends in what she found to be a welcoming and close-knit community. The people were neighbourly and looked out for one another. The place had a nice, old-fashioned, even quaint, feel to it. She settled in fast.

But now Michelle was angry. She didn't think about politics much but had been thinking hard since we had first talked in the focus group the evening before and had worked herself up into a 'lather', she told me. She was angry about the run-down condition of 'Accy' generally, angry about the state of her street and, the more she thought about it, angry about the local council, who made her follow rigid and, to her mind, ridiculous rules that endangered her business. 'Constantly checking the fridge temperature and looking for dirt on the work surfaces – which, as you can see, are spotless.' She ran her hand over the shiny Formica and rolled her eyes to heaven. She was also angry about the very high business taxes she paid to the council to take the shop's rubbish away: 'Commercial waste, they call it.' Adding insult to injury, she was quite sure that other business owners got off more lightly. Her frustration spilled over: 'I know a bloke with a corner shop who has mice running all over his counters – they don't dare go for him in case he plays the race card, so he doesn't even get checked.' Michelle, like many Red Wallers I met, sometimes felt convinced that she was being treated unfairly as a result of 'political correctness', with the council turning a blind eye to others' misdemeanours.

In the fifteen years since she moved to Accy, Michelle had watched the area go downhill fast. Factories were closing, good jobs were scarce, and the local town centre now had more shops boarded up than open for business. There was nowhere nice to go in the evening any more because so many of the city centre pubs were now doing a more lucrative trade in illegal drugs than in booze, she told me. Drugs were both a symptom and a cause of the town's problems. Michelle's theory was that the council used substance abuse as an 'earner', taking advantage of the low property prices and taking in addicts from other areas, housing and treating them for a fee.

Michelle was a worker. She had worked hard, really hard, all her life: 'I always have, I was brought up to believe you worked for what you got.' Her deepest resentment was reserved for people who could work but chose instead to live on benefits. She told me that single mothers with babies were housed further down the street, not bothering to look for work and setting, she believed, a bad example to their children. She compared these mums with Kayla, her assistant, a shy 32-year-old who could easily have been ten years younger. Kayla juggled her three days a week for Michelle with caring for five children and stepchildren, aged three to eighteen. Kayla's biggest worry was the lack of things to do for the older kids: 'God knows what they get up to! Maybe I'd rather not know.'

Trade had always been brisk at Michelle's butty shop, but now, like many others locally, her business had been hard hit by the switch in universal credit payments from weekly to monthly. Michelle knew exactly when it was paid out – she'd be crazily busy for a week, then 'bump! Nothing at all.' The Resolution Foundation's Blue Wall study backs this up, noting that the Red Wall has more working-age welfare spending than other areas and is 'therefore more vulnerable to changes in benefit generosity as a result'. This means that communities like Hyndburn are much more exposed to benefit cuts and therefore more likely to lose out significantly from the move to universal credit. For example, they suggest introducing universal credit will leave nearly 10 per cent more claimants in the north, the Midlands and Wales worse off, compared with claimants in London and the south-east – i.e. a lot of people. The impact is harsher still when individual cases are considered: a young single parent in a newly Tory Red Wall constituency will be £280 a year worse off, compared to their counterparts in other areas who will be £170–80 worse off.

I had arrived in Accrington the afternoon before my visit to Michelle and her cafe. The minicab driver who took me to the hotel was wearing shalwar kameez and a cloth cap. He told me how much he loved living in Accrington. As well as enthusiastically confirming Michelle's observations on the local property market, he told me that Accrington was really friendly, a 'no stress' place to live. Certainly he was on amicable terms with most other cabbies, including those working for rival firms, winding down the window and chatting and joking in Urdu when we pulled up alongside them at traffic lights. The area had been good to him and his family. His three grown-up children were all doing well: a daughter and son were both living locally and working as teachers, while the other son now lived in Blackburn and worked for Barclays bank. 'Good jobs, good futures,' he told me proudly. It was probably the most positive story I heard that day.

The Hyndburn constituency in Lancashire (not that anyone calls it Hyndburn: 'It's just a name that the council made up – we're Accy!') is formed from a cluster of former mill towns including Accrington, Oswaldtwistle, Great Harwood and Clayton-le-Moors. Created in 1983 when the Tories won it by just twenty-one votes, it has been Labour since 1992, with Graham Jones, a local man born and bred in the area, as its MP since 2005. On 12 December Jones was ousted by Sara Britcliffe, just twenty-four years old, also born and bred in the constituency, who had previously managed a shop in Oswaldtwistle. Sara (pronounced 'Saaara' one local told me, with a mock-posh flourish) is well known locally; in fact, she's almost Hyndburn aristocracy. Her father was the mayor on Hyndburn Borough Council and, before becoming the Tory candidate, she served as councillor in his old ward of St Andrews. She won a majority of 2,951 on a turnout of 59.8 per cent. The swing towards her was an impressive 9.9 per cent.

Britcliffe has squeezed an impressive amount into a short number of years. As well as serving as a councillor herself, getting up at 5 a.m. every day to commute to Manchester University where she studied modern languages, she was also lady mayoress when her father, Peter, became mayor in 2017. This was because her mother, Gabrielle Kroger, died tragically when Sara was just nine years old. As she told me when I interviewed her towards the end of April, 'I need to prove myself because of my age. I've had to work extremely hard – and to the people who ask if

I've had enough life experience to do the job I say, "I've had more life experience than I should have had at my age."' Britcliffe had made history the day before we spoke by being the first ever MP to make their maiden speech virtually, due to the coronavirus. In her speech she made a personal reference to the constituency's substance abuse problems that Michelle had talked about, mentioning her own mother's death from the 'devastating impact of alcoholism and mental health problems'. She also talked about her intention to fight for 'boosting funds for the north', saying this must not be a 'one-off response to the election' and warning ministers that, in the pursuit of this, she was determined to be, in Ken Clarke's words, 'a bloody difficult woman'.

I kicked off all the focus groups I ran in the Red Wall by asking participants to tell me what they liked most and least about the local area. Back in February, voters in Hyndburn found it easy to share their bugbears, shouting over each other, 'run down!', 'depressing!', 'down at heel!', 'no decent shops!', 'kids on street corners!', 'break-ins!' It took longer to tease out the things they liked beyond it being cheap, which was probably the most frequently cited attribute and didn't just refer to property: 'The same things in Aldi actually cost less here than they do in Manchester.' Some liked the sense of community, many of their friends and family living within a couple of streets: 'I never go much further than my friend's house, my daughter's and my son's.' There is a strong sense of it being a tight-knit area. Everyone knows each other's business and they all keep an eye on the people who need looking out for. It's 'old-fashioned, but in a good way', one of the women observed.

In our interviews, both the new MP and the former talked a lot about the people: Sara Britcliffe spoke about the 'strong values. We're down to earth here, with a hard work ethic.' She feels that the deep-rooted spirit and closeness is what makes the constituency special. Graham Jones agrees that 'community means everything to people in Accrington – which means they can take a while to trust outsiders. They are also the warmest and most generous, but responsibility and a commitment to the community remain the cornerstones of life up here.'

As the sessions wore on, more grievances emerged. The cheap cost of living came at a price. Accrington was once a major centre for the cotton and textile machinery industries. You can see a tall chimney stack from almost every street corner and many of the beautiful old mills are still standing, although most are now boarded up, out of use. Accrington was once famous for producing the hardest bricks in the world. Former MP Graham Jones sighed deeply when I asked about this, saying: 'Those brickworks have opened and closed so many times that you can't keep up with it.' The men could have spent the whole focus group session bemoaning the lack of employment. Almost all of them had been forced to travel. Ian had worked as far away as Birmingham: 'There's just not a lot going round here, compared with Birmingham. They have so much to do there. Go down and see all the stuff they have. I like the community here but I can see why people go to big cities.' Robert, a demolition site manager, also travelled: 'With my trade there's nothing much here. I have to work in Salford – it's a large American company. There's nothing like that here.'

Another major complaint was the poor quality of the town centre. Most said they hardly went there, preferring instead to drive to nearby Blackburn or even Manchester, or to shop online. The men were both amused and irritated by the council's recent resurfacing of the entrance to the Arndale Centre. 'It looks like someone's stuck cornflakes in the Tarmac,' Irfan told me to roars of laughter. It was a well-rehearsed local joke. I went there the next day. They were right: bright yellow flakes were scattered in the freshly laid black tarmac. No one was very sure how much it had cost, but it seemed to them to be another example of the local government's misplaced priorities. Some of the irritation lay in the fact that it had just appeared, replacing what several thought was expensive granite flooring, without explanation or consultation. 'No one ever asks us,' grumbled Andrew, a self-employed mechanic.

A much bigger blow for the women was the recent closure of Marks & Spencer. 'There's nothing nice here any more,' 'Nowhere to get something special – nowhere for presents,' 'Nowhere with good-quality things – nice knickers.' I was struck by the powerful impact of the loss of M&S as the pollster Peter Kellner had sent me an interesting article a few months before, pointing out how M&S store closures in small towns could be mapped closely to the Brexit-voting seats that Labour lost. He suggested that we might think of M&S as the canary in the mine, an early prediction of future demise in towns that have lost their sense of purpose. Certainly, the women in Accrington that blowy February night saw it as a symbol of the emptying out of the heart of their place, leaving little that they valued: 'Just tat and junk shops and pound stores and kebab bars.' Sara Britcliffe made the same point, adding her perspective as a young shopper. She felt that the centre had declined even in her short life and that it was important to give people more incentive to start their own businesses. Going to town with her friends ten years ago, there was so much more for young people – a New Look, for example. Now, there was nothing. No wonder most Hyndburn voters felt they had little reason to go to the town centre any more, leaving it to be colonised by aimless, out-of-control kids, homeless people, beggars and addicts.

Kenneth, the retired caravan club enthusiast who I visited in his neat two-up, two-down in Oswaldtwistle the next day, made the same point. As a butcher working in retail most of his working life, he had had a bird's-eye view of the changing fortunes of the town. For many years he managed a stall in Accrington's lovely Market Hall on Peel Street. When his boss closed the stall and opened a shop round the corner, he worked there instead. He blamed the shop's eventual closure partly on cheaper supermarkets opening up dotted around town, drawing life – and cash – out of the centre. But he also blamed people accepting lower quality meat: 'The council allowed a meat hawking van into the town centre,' he told me. 'Terrible meat but really, really cheap. If that's what people wanted; we just couldn't compete.' His pre-retirement years were spent making office furniture for Senator International, now the biggest local employer. 'I started with "peds" [pedestals that sit under desks] then moved up to the desks themselves.' He felt he had been very lucky to get another job given his age when the butcher shop folded, but he still missed being a butcher: butchery was always his first love. He tapped his chest as he spoke: 'It's in here, you see.'

Ken's home is the same house in which he started married life forty-seven years ago but, now divorced, he shares it with his dog, a friendly, tail-wagging Patterdale Terrier called Tod: 'I was still working when I got him, so he used to be on his tod.' He eventually took early retirement from Senator at sixty-two, and now keeps himself busy with fly fishing, with his allotment and as chairman and site manager of the local caravan club. He had become free at short notice on the day we met because Storm Dennis ('Dennis the Menace!') meant he had to cancel the caravan rally he was organising for that weekend: 'Bloody health and safety!' Ken, fond of the outdoors life, seemed more content living in the area than many of the people I heard from. Stepping into the street outside his house, if you look left you can see the beautiful Oswaldtwistle Moor where he walks Tod most days, while weekends are spent in the caravan in the local countryside, weather permitting. Life was good.

Others were far less positive. In the focus group the night before, Gary, a boxing instructor, had bemoaned the lack of night life. Apparently, Sunday night in Accy used to be a thing. Clubbers would descend on the town centre from all around the region; the Town Hall square would be buzzing. The younger men in the focus group talked enthusiastically about this local attraction that sprang out of nowhere but, sadly, disappeared almost as fast. No one knows why the Sunday night clubbers don't come any more. The town centre is as dead at night as it is during the day. The men in my focus group were particularly upset by how many pubs have shut down. Gordon, a retired electrician who likes a drop of real ale, told me that you could no longer find a decent pint anywhere in the town. Like Michelle, many were convinced that those pubs that have stayed open are now no-go areas – their most likely customers would be drug dealers and addicts. Few bother to go, and those with kids or grandkids are worried about them mixing with the wrong types.

In some ways, the biggest downside of the Hyndburn constituency is how hard it is to get away. Public transport links are poor, making it hard to work, shop or use the superior leisure facilities of nearby towns and cities. Manchester, although just twenty-five miles away, takes an hour and twenty minutes to get to by train. Most people drive to get anywhere – the motorways are good, some told me. Free car parking was one of the most popular items on everyone's wish-list, and the cost of petrol a big feature in any conversation about budget. The Resolution Foundation found that workers in the Red Wall are unlikely to commute by train (just 2 per cent do) and are more likely to travel by car than any other group in the country.

One of Kenneth's children had moved to Manchester and he talked about this with enormous regret, as if his son had moved to Australia. Like many of the people I spoke to, he felt conflicted between wanting a better future for his children and wanting them to remain nearby, part of this close-knit community. Sadly, it seems that, right now, having both is not possible if you live in Hyndburn.

Country Durham's position within England.

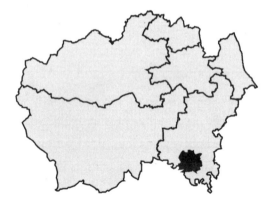

Darlington's position within County Durham.

4

DARLINGTON

'We've been through a few ups and downs,
but it feels like we're on the up here now...'

I was born in Darlington and lived there until I was seven, when my dad's job at Barclays bank took our family 'down south'. I hadn't been back since my granny died, when I was in my late teens. Arriving at the station on a warm and sunny March morning several decades later, I remembered a long-forgotten childhood ritual: showing off the iconic Locomotion No. 1, Britain's first ever passenger-carrying steam train, to visiting family and friends. The engine had been displayed at the station for years after Joseph Pease, the local Quaker benefactor, had paid £50 to restore it when it reached the end of its working life. He believed it belonged in Darlington, and had it mounted on a plinth outside the station. When my family met visiting relatives and friends there, this was our first stop as we introduced our town to newcomers.

The engine later moved down the road to Darlington's Head of Steam museum and is now the subject of a controversial proposal to move it to the Locomotion Museum in Shildon (where my own grandfather worked as a railways clerk). Darlington is not happy. The new MP Peter Gibson has joined council leader Heather Scott in calls to ensure the train, 'the jewel in our railway heritage crown', stays put. Meanwhile Matthew Pease, Joseph's great-great-great-grandson, has demanded that his ancestor's wishes be honoured.

Darlington – 'Darlo' to many locals – is rightly proud of its heritage and has something of a track record in safe-guarding it. The first person I met there was Yvonne Richardson, a local activist who campaigned tirelessly, and, as it turned out, successfully, to save the local library – also a gift to the town by the Pease family in 1885 – from the then Labour council's plans to close it down. Yvonne was wearing a tiny silver badge depicting Locomotion No. 1 on the collar of her jacket, which she proudly showed me as we sat down to chat.

We perched on tiny chairs round a tiny table in the children's section of the library, watched by a cheery cartoon dragon painted into a mural at the end of the room. She told me how she, a 71-year-old grandmother, had become involved in the campaign and how it had shaped her views on politics and politicians. Yvonne, as she explained, was not Darlington born and bred but had moved there from Durham when her children left home: 'I just fancied a change of scene.' She'd always liked Darlington. She told me she was self-educated – 'I left school at fifteen with no qualifications' – and talked passionately about libraries as a tool for educating working-class people. She was particularly passionate about this one, originally known as the 'Free Library'. Looking around I could see why: it's a beautiful Grade II-listed building, now boasting a well-equipped, and evidently well-used, computer room, a large reference library and even a small art gallery showing local artwork that features highlights of the town, including a mocked-up travel poster imploring tourists to visit 'Monte Darlo'.

Back in 2016, Yvonne had been horrified to discover the council's plans to close the building down. They planned to maintain a streamlined library service (the 1964 Public Libraries and Museums Act states that councils have a statutory duty to provide libraries), but to move it to the nearby Dolphin Sports Centre. While she understood that councils were having to manage savage cuts, after visiting the proposed new site she concluded it was wholly inadequate. More than that, she was sad about the loss of the library building itself, with its elegant domed ceilings, stained glass, panelled walls and beams and tailormade bookshelves. This blow came on the back of the closure of the much-loved Darlington Arts Centre, 'still a stab in the heart'. Yvonne set up a Facebook page and the local campaigning group, Darlington for Culture, got involved too. They organised a large demonstration. 'I'd never seen anything like it,' she said. 'There were hundreds of people in the street outside here, then we all met in the square.' They lobbied the council after developing an alternative business plan to make the library self-funding. She and the group were disappointed at the response from the Labour council. They approached Jenny Chapman, then Labour MP, who explained that, as MP, her scope for challenging the council's decision was limited. This was also deeply disappointing.

Yvonne has a theory about what happened here, believing that the 'Labour elite' had quickly closed ranks, leaving her outside. Her tone remained calm and measured as she explained her thinking, but her words betrayed her resentment. 'We're just the little people,' she told me,

> I've had no education – I was self-educated. Who am I? I was the most prominent person on the campaign, it turns out – where were the great and the good? Where were the politicians? Where was the Rotary Club? All the people who network? Nowhere to be seen. Why? You tell me! I've got my theories, but what do I know? I think it's because of the way that Labour works. If you're an educated person you're part of that socialist tribe and to me it feels tribal.

She felt let down by the council and, though she liked Chapman and believed her to be sincere about wanting to keep the library, she was frustrated that the local MP had so little power to make things happen.

The breakthrough in saving her beloved library came when Peter Cuthbertson, the prospective Tory candidate in the forthcoming 2017 election, got in touch out of the blue. He introduced Yvonne's group to a lawyer who had worked on similar cases, and, together, they decided to mount a legal challenge. The legal review failed, as did Cuthbertson's 2017 attempt at winning the Darlington constituency for the Tories – days before the election the national media unearthed blog posts from his past asserting some questionable beliefs: that a woman's sexual history is relevant in alleged rape cases; that more guns would improve morality in society; and heralding a 'courageous' priest in Sweden for preaching against homosexuality. Despite this election game-changer, he improved his share of the vote by 8 per cent, though still lost by some 3,000 votes. It was the end of the road for Cuthbertson's career, but his intervention had breathed new life into the library campaign, propelling it into the public's notice.

In September 2018, a few months ahead of 2019 local elections, new council leader Stephen Harker reversed the previous leader's decision and awarded £2 million to restore the library building. The move was not enough to save Labour in the council elections that May. The incoming Tory administration went further, upping Labour's last-minute pledge by a further £800k. The library was well and truly saved. Yvonne told me that this episode had 'opened her eyes to politics'. When I asked how – and how this has impacted on her own voting behaviour – she explained that switching to the Conservatives from Labour was not difficult: the Tories had been much more receptive to her campaign, but it wasn't just that. This was proof that the Tories listened to voters much more carefully than

Labour did. Labour's attitude, she felt, was paternalistic: we know best, we know what's good for you better than you do. In fact, Brexit, she told me, rather than the library, was the best example of this. People like her, the 'little people', were fed up with not being listened to.

In the focus groups that I ran later the same day, the library did not come up spontaneously. On prompting, some were aware that there had been a battle, and although few ever went there, everyone seemed pleased that the building had survived and was fulfilling its original purpose. There was a strong sense of pride in Darlington and its heritage, which was well known. The room we sat in, in the refurbished Kings Hotel, overlooked the statue of Joseph Pease that faces toward the market square, and, waiting for the first focus group to settle in, several of the women pointed him out to me and talked knowledgeably about the town's relationship with the Pease family. Most of the people I listened to were pretty positive about the town and what it had to offer. Some were Darlo born and bred but others, like Yvonne, had made an active choice to move there – a choice that they were mainly happy with.

Bob, a 58-year-old handyman, had moved to Darlington from Scotland as a young man when he left the army, following his parents, who had moved there too. He began working in the family's newsagent business, then briefly as a taxi driver, though he found that 'it wasn't for me, too much sitting in a cab'. This was followed by some years working at various jobs in the manufacturing sector, firstly for Flymo, a role that ended when the company sold the contract he was working on to the US. He then spent fourteen years in a factory in Crook, making components for freezers. This went well: he became a shift manager and went to college on day release, but eventually an American firm took over the company and all the manufacturing shifted to Turkey. After some months job hunting – 'I got down to the last six seven times' – he drew a blank and instead turned his hand to painting and decorating. He still lived in the same house in the same quiet close that he had lived in for twenty years, and kept himself busy volunteering as a youth worker, spending some years drawing on his army background helping with the cadets and then, more recently, with the boy scouts. He says Darlington is a nice place to live, 'just the right size, friendly, not too big, not too small'.

Most of the people I spoke to shared Bob's analysis of Darlington: a decent-sized town untroubled by the bustle and anonymity of a larger city but still with adequate amenities. Jenny Chapman had anticipated that I would hear grumbles about the lack of shops, and while there was some disappointment from the women I spoke to that some bigger stores had closed down – especially the totemic M&S – most felt that this was no worse than many other places and that Darlington had fared much better than other nearby towns. Malcolm, a retired prison officer, claimed that Darlington was 'much nicer than Redcar, Middlesbrough or Stockton'. He had visited Stockton recently for the first time in years and was shocked: 'I thought, what's happened here? It's gone downhill fast. Shabby-looking. Shops closing down. Only charity shops and cash converters left.' He noticed people he saw on the streets looking at him with recognition and realised this was because they were ex-prisoners he had last come across when working.

Chapman had also anticipated, this time rightly, that the town's vibrant night life would come in for praise: 'Sometimes you see more people out and about on a Saturday night than you do during the day.' The increasing number of independent shops was a positive too: 'They're fantastic and it really gives you hope.' Chapman had wondered, though, if there would be concern about the increasing number of out-of-town shopping centres, with their potential to draw energy from the centre. I found that, while people value the centre and want it to improve, they also welcomed the proliferation of further-afield 'clusters', as Gaynor, a baker specialising in pastries at local chain Cooplands, described them. She talked enthusiastically about this improvement: 'It's getting so much better, everything used to be in the centre of town but now you've got Iceland on the North Road, Morrisons on the Yarm Road, clusters all over Darlington. If you are a pensioner without a car you can get the bus to your nearest cluster.' Notably, while M&S, amongst others, have abandoned the high street, they do have a presence out of town.

There was also a feeling that, while having been through some difficult times, with its manufacturing industry in decline for some twenty years, Darlington was now enjoying a period of revival. Some jobs had been saved and a strong service sector had been introduced, with new jobs created in finance, communications and through the new Amazon delivery centre. Mick, who works for a kitchen company, felt that Darlington had benefited from significant investment in recent years. Bob had been a victim of the industrial decline, being made redundant twice. But since setting himself up as a painter and decorator, he's never looked back: 'Business is great – I'm turning stuff down. It's grown by word of mouth. Folk seem to like what I do and recommend me. Really can't complain at all.' Most of the men, like Mick, felt reasonably well-off, although the women, more likely to be working part-time in low-paid caring, retail and cleaning jobs, were less comfortable. Julie, a grandmother of two whose time is taken up helping with childcare and dog-sitting, had been made redundant from her job in an animal welfare charity and now worked a few nights a week as a cleaner at a local gym. It is, she explained, mainly for 'pocket money', as her husband, a retired public sector worker, had a reasonably generous pension.

I had to push for negatives or things people would like to see change. There was some concern about the younger generation: many felt that children were now brought up very differently to how they themselves had been brought up and that this resulted in lack of respect, an expectation of 'getting something for nothing'. Mick felt that kids wanted to have 'the celebrity lifestyle, with their iPhones and everything', but that too often they didn't want to work for it: 'They just expect it all to be there.' HGV driver Phil agreed but felt that his generation was partly to blame; they were less strict than their parents had been: 'We gave them everything … and spoilt them rotten.' There was a general view that things had changed: 'It was a different world when we were young – we were all down the pits or the quarries – everyone was the same and had the same expectations, but now it's different.' Ronnie, an electrician, felt that their generation had changed more than they realised: 'We've moved on too – our values and morals may be the same, but we all own our own homes. Our parents never dreamt of that.' Mick agreed: 'Yes, and we all want the latest sixty-inch screen. We used to just pay the BBC licence and now it's Sky this, Netflix that, broadband that. There are that many bills going out that it's hard to keep up.'

There was some sympathy for the next generation too: many felt that, pleasant though Darlington is, it has little to offer for young people to do. While that doesn't excuse the anti-social behaviour or drugs that some felt are on the increase, it doesn't help. The women felt this particularly strongly, bemoaning the lack of open spaces: 'They took away the parks for kids, and now there's only one skate park.' Many talked about the lack of youth clubs: 'The Dolphin Centre used to be OK but it's so scruffy and run-down now.' The few youth programmes that are left depend on volunteers. Bob reminded everyone about Top Deck:

You know it, it used to be at the top of Victoria Road. It was a well-run church youth club but the lady who set it up and ran it for years was seventy-seven years old. It was always packed, the kids loved it, but when she wanted to retire finally she couldn't find anyone to take it on and the whole thing closed down.

Several were concerned about drugs that young people turned to in the absence of anything else: 'In our day under-age drinking was as bad as it got, but now...' Some linked this to what they saw as a growth of crime. While 'most people were mostly on minor stuff – weed and that, you can smell it everywhere', some felt that there was something more sinister at play: 'There are gangs. I've been burgled three times – all drugs-related and my work van was done twice for tools,' Bob complained.

When asked who might be able to bring about the changes they wanted to see, the start point for most was the council. There was some awareness that the council had changed political hands recently but also confusion about what the council is responsible for and what the MP is responsible for. Some thought that Peter Gibson, the new Tory MP, was the council leader. Jenny Chapman, the long-standing Labour MP who lost in December, was also thought by some to have been council leader. Chapman was, on the whole, well known and well liked, especially by the women in my focus groups, who were impressed by an initiative she had championed whereby she put out a call for unwanted second-hand school uniforms, personally removed the name tags and then offered them to families who were struggling to afford uniforms for their kids.

'She was rooted in the community and did a lot of things like that – all off her own back – just to help people.' No longer voting Labour was not, they were clear, a reflection on her, but rather a reflection of their wholesale rejection of the party. Sue, a qualified sewing machinist who worked in the haberdashery at Boyes, a family-run department store ('If you can't get it in Boyes, you don't need it'), told me: 'They thought we'd always vote Labour – we'd always be their little puppets. They just took it for granted that everyone up north would vote Labour. Well, they were wrong.'

This sentiment was very familiar to Jenny Chapman. She told me that she'd heard it again and again on the doorstep. 'People who had voted Labour for years were so bloody angry and wanted to give us a real kicking.' She recognised the view that the party was out of tune with its most loyal voters: 'They didn't think we gave a toss about people like them.' She talked about voters' frustration with the state of the Labour Party, describing it as 'lawless, like an out-of-control car careering downhill knocking things over'. She also detailed her own frustration as a popular local MP, powerless to criticise or bring about the change that people wanted to see:

> They were angry with me that I didn't support him [Jeremy Corbyn] but hadn't managed to do anything. They felt Labour had to change and they were right. I argued but they knew I knew it. I've lived here forty-plus years. They know me. But they wanted to make sure that we got the message.

She still felt the warmth of personal affection, developed over years. 'Even during the election there was something about how they said it – like when you lose it with a child. We've had our telling and we've earned a crushing defeat. But afterwards people were warm and affectionate and just lovely. They put their arm around you.'

Chapman is convinced that Darlington is now willing Labour on, but incoming Tory MP Peter Gibson is not so sure. He describes Darlington as a 'bellwether' seat rather than part of the traditional Red Wall, a seat that, though historically tending towards Labour, falls to whichever party has a significant majority. He believes that Labour had become complacent locally and nationally, 'disinterested and disassociated from the public'. He felt that the town was looking for someone to champion their corner, and told me about his campaign to obtain extra funding for Darlington station, which was now at capacity: 'We can't run an extra single line so I'm bidding for £73 million for two extra platforms and to improve parking.' A couple of weeks after we spoke, in March 2020 Rishi Sunak's first Budget granted this funding, giving Gibson a quick win. Gibson believes the Tories' national campaign succeeded because it was positive, and he tried to echo this in Darlington.

I can sum it up like this: it didn't appear in my leaflets but I what I wanted to do was 'make Darlington great again'. That feeling resonates with people. If you say just vote for me and get four years of the same, it won't bring people to you. You have to say, 'I'm going to be really positive about our town. I'm going to fight every step of the way asking for more investment, more jobs, to show people who we are and how this is one of the best places to be.' Even a small inkling of local pride will gee you up, fire you up, inspire you and you'll think, 'This is the person who will stand up for us and do something positive for the area.'

Gibson talked about the importance of Boris Johnson's positivity, but early in our interview another Tory politician came up, one whose election Gibson described as 'momentous', and who, perhaps more than any other, he feels paved the way for his own election victory: Ben Houchen, mayor for Tees Valley since 2017. It is unusual for a local politician to make the kind of impact that Houchen, a locally born, rugby-playing lawyer, has but I found that most voters I spoke to could not only name him but could also trot out a list of his achievements: 'The airport was going to rack and ruin but he has brought it back to life – they now have so many more flights: to Alicante, Amsterdam, you name it.' He has also pulled off a deal buying back land from Tata Steel as part of his South Tees Development Corporation project. The aim is to create 20,000 new jobs and to contribute £1 billion to the UK economy per year. These goals are well known, and successes so far suggest that the bold ambition might just be realised. As Phil explained, Houchen's commitment to the area had helped Phil overcome both his scepticism about its future and his scepticism about Conservative politicians: 'I do have my doubts. But he's got the vision. And he's made some progress that you can actually see. Not just talking, getting on with it, getting everyone in and working together. It's inspiring. He believes in the area, and I believe in him.'

Staffordshire's position within England.

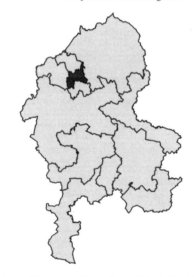

Stoke-on-Trent Central's position within Staffordshire.

5

STOKE-ON-TRENT

'Stoke will suffer after all this. Ordinary working-class people will suffer. We'll come out worse; we always do.'

Stoke-on-Trent was the last constituency that I was due to visit, towards the end of April 2020. The mood felt very different because, by then, with the whole country in lockdown, Covid-19 dominated the conversation. Problems that might have seemed a high priority just weeks before suddenly seemed to pale into insignificance. Even the way I carried out the fieldwork was different. My focus groups had to be online rather than face to face. In the early days of people grappling with online interactions there were practical problems with this. Eddie, a 67-year-old sales assistant, Barbara, a 61-year-old care worker, and Nina, retired in her late fifties, all tried and failed to dial in to the session. Maria, a shop assistant in her early fifties, had borrowed her daughter's laptop but couldn't quite figure it out and her image dangled sideways on the screen for the duration of our session. Justine, a forty-year-old PA, had very poor Wi-Fi and kept freezing and cutting out. Even when it was working well she sounded like a Dalek. These are problems that everyone reading will be very familiar with after spending weeks doing virtual meetings and virtual socialising – and, of course, as the weeks went by we all got much better at it – but it was frustrating nonetheless.

Still, the sometimes clunky technology couldn't hide the sheer ebullience of the Stokies' enthusiasm for their home town. It can be hard to manage group dynamics online, as anyone who has ever tried to chair a lockdown meeting will know all too well. It's even harder with a lively group of people from Stoke-on-Trent eager to tell you about what's special about their place. I heard a lot about Stoke City football club, about Stoke – or Staffordshire – oatcakes. They're 'like a sort of fat pancake – I have them every day for breakfast – delicious!' said Ronnie, a bus driver whose job in more normal times is to drive people to another local attraction that came in for a few positive mentions: Alton Towers. Most of all, though, I heard about the Stokies themselves – for it seems that the most special thing about Stoke-on-Trent is the people who live there. When I asked the focus groups to describe Stoke in a few words, I was met with a torrent of positives: 'strong community', 'lovely people', 'friendly, nice and helpful', 'hard-working, passionate, colourful'. Almost everybody I met had been born and bred in Stoke – and the handful who had left for work or college had all chosen to return. Several told me how they absolutely loved living there and others told me that they would never, ever leave.

This passionate sense of belonging set the people of Stoke-on-Trent somewhat apart from those of Hyndburn and Darlington. Yet there were strong similarities with other Red Wall places too. Stoke, like everywhere I visited, has a proud past that its people very much regard as their own personal history. Everyone I spoke to had a parent or grandparent who had worked in a pot bank, the local name for a pottery factory. The saying goes that Stokies have 'slip in their veins', referring to the liquid clay used in traditional pottery making. That may be true, but no one I met works there now. My focus group participants were typical of other Red Wall locations: care workers, classroom assistants, brickies, electricians, shopworkers, drivers and hairdressers. It's unsurprising, since the potteries, employing more than 70,000 people in the 1950s, now employ just 6,000. Of course, many of the great names still exist, but they have shifted production abroad: Wedgwood and its subsidiary Royal Doulton now manufacture in Indonesia. This doesn't stop the people of Stoke from feeling that the potteries belong to them. Former Labour MP Gareth Snell told me, 'If a Stokie goes out for a meal they'll always turn the plate over to see if it's made in Stoke.' However, as in other places I visited, this pride sits alongside a deep sense of loss.

I explained why I was running the session online and that I was disappointed not to visit Stoke as I hadn't been for years – my last visit had been with my own family as a teenager and I remembered visiting a pot bank and watching pottery being made. The women's focus group explained that such a trip just wouldn't be possible now – all that is left are museums showing how things used to be. Karen, an admin assistant in a special school, told me what was by now a very familiar Red Wall story of the impact of industrial decline: 'The potteries have all gone now, the collieries have all gone now. All our families would have likely worked in one or the other. That's why we've got such a loss of identity.' Others embellished Karen's story, talking about the run-down nature of the area, the poverty and deprivation, the homelessness, the food banks, the derelict buildings, the empty shops. Pete, a sales assistant for a mobile phone company, though currently furloughed on 80 per cent wages, observed that building projects often don't get finished: 'Things are never followed through. They start the build then I suppose they run out of money. Stoke is full of dangerous half-finished blocks. They're an eye sore,' he complained. Hanley, I was told, once the thriving heart of the area's industry and still the biggest commercial centre in the area, is now a 'no-go' area, especially at night. 'It's horrendous, really run-down – a lot of poverty,' added Jean, a care worker in the local hospital.

I heard about the new industries that had replaced the old ones. Stoke is emerging as an important 'distribution centre', its geographical location and good transport connections, especially its proximity to the M6, mean that Amazon, Screwfix and others have chosen it for warehousing, providing new jobs that are plentiful but generally low-skilled and low-paid. Gareth Snell pointed out that Stoke's weekly wage is £100 below the regional average and £125 below the national average. The biggest employer now is bet365, providing work for 4,000. Its offices were established on the site of the old steelworks. The Coates family seemed to get a good press: a family-run business that treats its workers well and pays a living wage. The firm had laid people off on full pay for the duration of lockdown and was thought to do its bit in the community. Jo Gideon, the Conservative MP newly elected in December 2019, told me that the very first time that she spoke in the House of Commons it was to defend bet365, and she had no issue at all with doing so: 'I've never found anyone with a bad thing to say about them. A taxi driver who picked me up at the station once told me that the happiest people that he drove around were the people who worked at bet365.'

Gideon thinks the strength of family businesses like bet365 reflects the strength of local families more generally. Gareth Snell also described the tight-knit community: 'When you're canvassing you knock on a door, then you go three doors down and you meet their auntie and then another two doors down and it's their grandma.' He told me that the principal of one of the schools in Bentilee – once the biggest council estate in Europe – had reported that he never had to worry about kids on snow days or on an occasion when the school had to be closed because of a burst pipe: 'The community would take the kids in. They would all go round to a neighbour's house. Someone would end up taking a dozen kids in because, quite simply, that's what they did.'

There was also ample evidence of local community action. Snell told me about St Stephen's Church, also in Bentilee: 'It's one of those places where you have effectively all the social services rolled into one.' And Gideon found that much of what she saw around her was reflecting back her Arnold Bennett lockdown reading: 'Stoke has a strong Methodist tradition. People don't have much and don't expect much.' She told me one of the most inspirational people she had met since being in Stoke was Danny Flynn, CEO of the North Staffs YMCA, who does valuable work in the community, including organising regular community meals that anyone can join in and share.

Another typical Red Wall feature was the Stokies' absolute fury at being 'left behind', missing out on the country's wealth – wealth that they feel their area played a significant part in generating. Justine, a forty-year-old PA, when we spoke furloughed and struggling with home-schooling her kids, agreed with the points others were making about 'loss of identity', but went further. She believed that Stoke had been 'robbed' of the prosperity it used to have and still richly deserved. The group of men picked up this theme even more, strongly bringing up the north-vs-south resentment that I had heard everywhere I went: 'We always miss out round here,' said one. Both groups talked disparagingly about the distribution centres that had sprung up everywhere: they are an inadequate substitute for the traditional industries they have replaced. 'We're just a park-and-ride for them – people pass through Stoke because we're convenient. But we're overlooked.' Others agreed that Stoke-on-Trent's main advantage in the eyes of the likes of Amazon is geographical convenience: 'We're a thoroughfare – a good place to travel through and out the other side,' grumbled Karen. 'They've picked us because we're in the middle – the middle of nowhere.'

Being overlooked is amplified because Stoke, they explained, isn't really a city. Instead it is six towns strung together: Stoke-on-Trent itself, the administrative centre; Hanley, where many of the people I spoke to lived, and universally declared (by them) to be 'a dump'; plus Burslem, Tunstall, Longton and the one Arnold Bennett left out in his novels: Fenton. There were debates about whether there actually was a centre and, if so, where that centre was. Either way, no one went there. When I asked people where they went to do shopping, I was told that shopping was done online – although for something special you might make the trip to Manchester. Jean, who lives on the outskirts of Hanley, said she hadn't been there for eleven months. The absence of an M&S had been an important symbol of decline in Hyndburn and Darlington, but the women in Stoke-on-Trent couldn't remember at first whether there was a local store or not. After discussion, the consensus was that Hanley did have an M&S, 'but it's one of the rubbish ones – nothing decent in it at all. Just old lady clothes. Nothing you'd want to buy.' I heard now-familiar resentment at the area's decline. There was also derision at what some saw as an attempt to 'window-dress' the area but without any actual cash being spent. Colin asked me if I knew what they called the part of town he'd been working in that morning. I didn't and he roared with laughter: 'The cultural quarter! Cultural quarter!'

he repeated, now in a mock-posh, southern accent. 'Do you know what's there? Nothing! Absolutely nothing! As if calling it a cultural quarter will make it cultural! What a joke!'

It seems that the people of Stoke have good reason to feel aggrieved. Gareth Snell told me, 'All too often, Stoke is at the top of every table that you want to be at the bottom of, and at the bottom of every table that you want to be at the top of.' Despite investment in the fabric of local schools, the stats report educational attainment falling well below average. In common with other Red Wall constituencies, few of the people I met were graduates. Also in common with other Red Wallers, the biggest worry for the parents and grandparents that I chatted to was what the future held for their kids, and this anxiety was woven through most of our discussion, particularly when the conversation focused on the loss of manufacturing industry and skills. 'I don't expect them to bring back the pits, but they could bring back the potteries to be more like they were,' suggested Jean. Like other Red Wall places too, there was little expectation – or desire – for their young people to move away from home. But that led to huge concern about what they were going to be able to do: 'There's nothing for them here now.' Jo Gideon echoed this concern, talking about the 'depressingly poor' life chances for young people. She told me she was determined to look at creating more apprenticeships: 'We can't give up on people when they reach sixteen.'

All my Stoke-on-Trent conversations started and finished with the overwhelming preoccupation of the day: Covid-19. While our discussion had ranged around hopes and expectations of a better future for the area following the election, many Stoke voters felt that these conversations were now irrelevant compared with the enormity of the task of managing the crisis. There was a sense that, for now, normal politics had to be put on hold, whatever your loyalties: 'We just have to get through this as best we can,' said Karen. 'We have to put politics aside.' Jo Gideon felt this too. She was frustrated as a new MP trying to get to know her new patch, now stuck in the tiny flat she had hastily rented when she arrived last September. 'I got elected and then it was very intense in Westminster getting the Withdrawal Bill through, then it was Christmas and now this. I miss being able to connect with people in the same room.' She also explained how she and other new Stoke MPs had collaborated to develop a local levelling-up plan: 'We three Stoke MPs working with Aaron Bell and Karen Bradley put together a North Staffs package, mainly about better transport links in the area, reinstating closed lines and stations – a sort of reverse Beeching. We've also looked at improving bus services. But the challenge now is: will that money be available?'

It was four weeks into lockdown when I first spoke to people in Stoke and, although they were broadly supportive of what the government had done so far, they were also aware of, and shared, criticisms of the government: being slow to announce lockdown in the first place; slow to get effective testing up and running; neglectful of care homes and the people who worked in and relied on them; and responsible for a catastrophic shortage of PPE. Jean was a care worker in the local hospital and had plenty to say about how poorly equipped it was: 'We have to use pillowcases to dry the patients. No dry wipes, no clean towels. It's a nightmare.' There was also some scepticism about how it was that money, previously not forthcoming as austerity hit the area, had suddenly been available. 'North Staffs got extra cash, which is great – but the staff there have been overstretched for ages – why didn't it happen before?' asked Karen. And Justine was scornful: 'For years there has been a shocking lack of funding and now it's miraculously available. How come?'

Perhaps the biggest worry stems from the long-standing belief that Stoke-on-Trent has been forgotten, neglected and left behind – and that the impact of the coronavirus will follow an invidious pattern. New MP Jo Gideon was mindful of this. Referring to the Conservatives' big idea for the Red Wall, which implies that those neglected constituencies will be raised up economically to the same standard as more fortunate areas, she observed:

> Levelling up is, in a way, more important than ever given the coronavirus crisis. It's not the same for everybody. It's much harder if you are in a tiny flat than if you are in a nice environment and you've got a garden. It's worse if you are in an abusive relationship, much harder if you have kids. Given coronavirus, there will be lots of short-term things that we need to look at, and if I can be a catalyst for highlighting the most important things here and can try to bring people together to work out solutions and deliver solutions – I think that's the main role of an MP.

The voters I spoke to in Stoke shared Gideon's concerns but took a gloomier view of the likely outcome. 'We've always been an after-thought, we're the poor relation – and we probably will be again,' predicted Karen. 'Stoke will suffer after all this. Ordinary working-class people will suffer. We'll come out worse; we always do.'

6

PRIDE, PLACE AND PATRIOTISM

'Even in the past fifteen years I've seen this place get worse and worse. But it's been going downhill much longer than that. You want to feel proud of it but it's a struggle, like you want to feel proud of your country but that's been a struggle too.'

Everywhere I visited in the Red Wall had a proud history, a history that told a positive story about the place and what made it special. Often it was about its industry and the distinctive skills that had evolved from that: Darlington's railways, Oswaldtwistle's mills, Stoke's potteries. All of the places were famous for something – if not several things – and the people I chatted to were often very knowledgeable. They were delighted to tell me about the work that their parents and grandparents used to do. I also heard a lot about each region's relationship with the country as a whole. This manifested itself in different ways too: through the place's military history, for example Hyndburn's Accrington Pals, or through the contribution that its specific industrial heritage made to Britain. But the pride drawn from this now is always nostalgic, almost entirely rooted in the past. I asked women in my focus group in Darlington what made them proud: 'Our heritage,' they told me. 'We've a lot of history round here.'

Looking around their towns now, many of the people I spoke to struggled to find examples of anything that could match its glorious past. Too often the overwhelming feeling was regret – even for Darlington, overall the most positive of my 'deep dive' locations and now considered by many of its residents to be 'on the up'. At best, people saw a failure to maintain a leading edge and fulfil the area's heady promise, but at worst, in Hyndburn for example, they saw only decay. The Social Fabric Project, launched in March by Onward, the cross-party campaigning think tank, confirms that these feelings of loss are widespread, but particularly powerful in the sorts of towns that make up the Red Wall. Quoting a recent survey by the UPP Foundation, they suggest that, while 30 per cent (still not high, admittedly) of people who live in cities believe that their area has improved, this drops to 22 per cent of people in large towns and just 17 per cent of people living in Red Wall-style small towns. BritainThinks' Mood of the Nation survey echoes this sense of social decline too, finding that the main reasons for the persistent cloud of pessimism hanging over the country included rising crime, the decline of the high street, and fewer places that people can meet and socialise.

Everyone told me how crime in their place was on the up. Notably, few talked about rising cybercrime and fraud, focusing instead on physical crime, the kind of crime that visibly blights a community: car theft and vandalism, burglary and break-ins and personal crime, particularly muggings. The Mood of the Nation survey found that an astonishing one-in-five of us expect that we or a close family member will be the victim of violent crime in the next year. This was often linked to perceptions of a growing drugs problem, with people describing town centres up and down the country as 'no-go' areas, especially at night. 'There are hardly any pubs nowadays, and those that are left aren't making their money out of drink; it's all about drugs,' complained call centre manager Ali in Accrington, while Celia grumbled that her street was 'being used as a dumping ground for recovering drunks and people in rehab. It's just got worse and worse. You see another To Let sign and you think, "Oh God, what's coming next?"' Voters in Darlington felt that their place was probably no worse than others but still felt that, as Bob put it, 'drugs are a massive issue … some big players are at it and it's behind most crimes that you see'. Jean in Stoke-on-Trent described the centre of Hanley as 'horrendous' and told me she had banned her children from going there at night when they were teenagers.

A lot of the talk focused less on serious crime and more on frequent, irritating anti-social behaviour, which people tended to blame on kids not having enough to do. People told me about intimidating groups of teenagers hanging about on street corners, about litter and graffiti, and about damage to local buildings, especially those that are derelict and boarded-up. Michelle pointed out several such buildings in her own street, which is, by her own description, 'pretty rough'. She reasoned, though, that 'if there isn't anything nice in the neighbourhood you can't really expect people to behave nicely and look after it, can you?' This tended to be something that worried women voters more than men, but almost everyone felt that this kind of low-level crime had spiralled out of control and had become low priority for the police, who were too short-staffed to even try to deal with it. Many linked it to their sense that young people nowadays lack respect (though all excused their own children and grandchildren from this judgement). Julie, whom I interviewed in her Darlington home, sighed as she told me that 'kids these days are arrogant with no respect for teachers and police'. She told me that the health visitor who helped her when her son was born some twenty-odd years before had predicted this development: 'She said that this generation would be coming through and that they would be trouble because she was seeing lots of single mums bringing up their kids quite happily to live on benefits.' I heard stories like this again and again, often connecting a perceived decline in standards and behaviour with reliance on welfare and poor parenting, especially from frequently criticised lone parents.

There was another explanation for negative change in Red Wallers' local area that I heard repeatedly: immigration. In 2010, in my first book, *Talking to a Brick Wall*, I wrote about how immigration had gradually emerged through the New Labour years as a 'vortex' issue, a lens through which the many grievances that voters identified could be explained. NHS overstretched? It's because of immigrants coming here to access our free care – it's the envy of the world. Schools underfunded? That's because immigrants turn up with their kids who can't speak English, meaning teachers have to spend too much time helping them. For workers, especially manual workers, the threat seemed very real. Immigration had risen to the top of the issues that voters were concerned about by the end of the last Labour government. It has now slipped back down the ranking, as the Oxford Migration Observatory found that the number of people mentioning it had dropped from 48 per cent in June 2016 to 13 per cent in November 2019. But this change seems to be largely because many have assumed that 'getting Brexit done' will also deal with the problem.

Certainly, immigration remains a powerful issue in the Red Wall seats I visited. It also emerged as one of the priority policy areas identified by Red Wall voters in the Labour Together citizens' jury. For these voters, with much to feel aggrieved about, resentment was never far from the surface. It seemed that they had more reason than most to look for an explanation for their misfortunes. Immigrant communities, familiar, visible, yet poorly understood, were often offered up as an answer. In Stoke-on-Trent, for instance, when I asked the focus group members to tell me about anything in the area that had changed for the worse, 'more ethnic groups in certain areas' came high up on the list and prompted discussion about the 'large Asian and Polish communities' who 'keep themselves to themselves'. As already discussed, several interviewees believed that the timing of the arrival of immigrant groups in their area coincided with its decline, despite the fact that most Red Wall constituencies have less immigration than other parts of the country.

Another topic that cropped up everywhere and was particularly troubling to the women I met was the decline of their high street. Of course, this is a widespread national problem – in BritainThinks' Mood of the Nation survey conducted months before Covid-19 made this prediction a reality, eight out of ten of us think that 'more shops will close than open in my local high street in the next year', but this felt particularly acute in the most neglected Red Wall towns. 'It's all chicken shops, kebab shops, charity shops and pound stores,' grumbled Ali, a young-looking grandmother of three. Jenny Chapman, the former MP for Darlington, feels that her town centre has suffered a crisis of identity in recent years. She observed that the centre 'looks old' when you go there – meaning that the people who frequented it were older Darlington citizens who didn't shop online and were not able or willing to drive to the larger shopping malls on the outskirts of the town. Although Binns, the town's long-standing House of Fraser department store, has had a recent stay of execution, in the past few years Darlington has lost BHS, Woolworths and M&S, to name just a few.

Then there is the loss of what think tank Onward describes as 'local assets': pubs, libraries, post offices and coffee shops. In Accrington I was often told how few pubs there are nowadays. Penny, a 42-year-old nursery nurse with a fourteen-year-old and a sixteen-year-old, could not imagine what her kids would be getting up to in a couple of years. It wasn't just the kids, though. As previously noted, Gary, a divorced personal trainer, bemoaned the lack of things to do in the evening and Michelle felt it was particularly difficult to meet people if you were older and single. According to Onward's analysis, the loss of British pubs is dramatic: the past twenty years have seen a decline from 52,500 to 38,850 – a drop of 26 per cent – with the sharpest drop being during the financial crisis, when more than 3,000 pubs were lost in a single year.

Libraries show a similar decline, again mentioned everywhere I went. Onward suggests that libraries have been lost faster than any other 'local asset': a 27 per cent drop from 4,392 in 2005 to 3,187 in 2018. The curve steepened as austerity kicked in and local councils have had to manage severe cuts. Darlington, although luckier in terms of its thriving night-time economy, has a particular history here, and I tell the story of local activist Yvonne Richardson's, successful campaign to save the city's beautiful library in Chapter 4. By her own admission, she and her campaign were lucky. Around the Red Wall, others will have been less so. Often housed in historic buildings – and often the gift of local dignitaries in happier times – the loss of such libraries, I think, is about more than the loss of a local asset or facility and, like the loss of M&S, takes on a greater importance as a symbol of the town's decay.

Of course, this decline has happened at a time when austerity has hit local councils hard everywhere, forcing deep and damaging cuts when there is greater than ever demand on some essential services. Social care, for example, is now estimated to be 38 per cent of a typical council's budget and is expected to rise up to 60 per cent in the next fifteen years. The Institute for Fiscal Studies estimates cuts of 21 per cent across the board since 2010. Research also shows that the Red Wall has been the hardest hit. The Centre for Cities think tank published a study in January 2020 showing that seven out of ten of the poorest communities are in the north of England: areas with higher poverty and weaker economies. It also shows that those areas have been affected by cuts twice as much as the more affluent south, with deeper cuts across the board but especially in areas like housing, planning, highways and transport, culture and youth services. Small wonder that many Red Wallers say their place has been neglected.

In the BritainThinks citizens' jury for Labour Together, we recruited people from the different Labour 'tribes': in one camp there were Leave voters who had abandoned Labour in 2019, recruited from Red Wall constituencies; and in the other were those we called 'urban Remainers', who had stuck with Labour. I was interested to see the contrast between people from Red Wall seats and the Urban Remainers. While the latter groups had chosen to live in their particular city, often leaving their hometown as a student or for work, Red Wallers were more likely to be born and bred in the town where they lived. While some had chosen to stay, many felt trapped in their place and helpless to act as they watched it decline. This led to acute feelings of frustration, even anger, contrasting with the contentment of Urban Remainers living in vibrant cities like London, Manchester or Birmingham. Urban Remainers tended to be very proud of the place they lived and the opportunities it offered. They felt that choosing to live there said something positive about them and they spoke about it with immense pride. Rory, a young solicitor in Manchester, was emphatic: 'Who doesn't love Manchester?! It's so diverse; it's the highest Remainer city! I moved here a few years ago and definitely consider it my home!' Hearing this, Simon, an accountant, observed, 'It sounds like London,' paying Manchester the biggest compliment he could think of.

By contrast, many Red Wallers often felt little connection with the largest city nearby, and many rarely went there. Hyndburn is only twenty miles from Manchester, but when Kenneth from Oswaldtwistle told me that his son had moved there he spoke as sadly as if he had moved half-way across the world. The people I spoke to in Stoke-on-Trent felt that their place was positioned in a corridor, hence its appeal as a distribution centre, but apart and separate from the nearest major city. Manchester would be visited for an occasional shopping trip, but there the connection ended. Darlington had an even more distant relationship with Durham or Newcastle. Sue, a shopworker, told me she'd be more likely to visit one of the retail clusters on the edge of town than venture further afield. Few had ever been to London: a focus of resentment for some. When I asked the men in Stoke if they would ever go to London to shop, Colin, a brickie, exploded, 'No way! They're not getting my money! They take enough from me as it is!'

If Red Wallers believe that their town is in decline and feel little sense of belonging either to nearby cities or the capital, it is perhaps not surprising that they look to the country as a source of pride. Red Wallers are strongly patriotic, much more so than voters living in other parts of the country. A BritainThinks survey in December 2018 found that people living in the northeast, Yorkshire and the Midlands were more than 10 per cent more likely to value being 'proud to be British' than people living in London. While the Urban Remainers group in our Labour Together citizens' jury developed straplines that spoke to fairness ('No One Left Behind' or 'Fairness for All') or looked to the future ('Tomorrow's Future Today'), the Red Wall group favoured 'Make Britain Great Again'. Graham Jones, the former MP for Hyndburn, talked about how important this was as a priority for his area: 'Community matters to people round here, but when they think about community they're thinking about the whole country. Their patriotism means that the country is what happens on their own doorstep and what happens on their own doorstep is the country.' When I interviewed Julie, a part-time cleaner, in her neat semi-detached home set back from the road in a Darlington suburb, she agreed with this. Her own patriotism focused on our 'wonderful heritage, including the royals – I don't care what anyone says, they do good work'. She also felt that our sense of community, 'especially up here in the north, is uniquely British. We'll all help each other out when needed, that's the nice thing about the British people.' She valued Britain's historic place in world too, but felt this is now sadly diminished: 'I mean we used to own the world, didn't we? The Commonwealth. We were a force to be reckoned with.' As I wrote up notes from Julie's interview some weeks later, I wondered what she would have made of the debate about the legacy of the Empire and Commonwealth that now dominated the news – especially Prince Harry and Meghan Markle's criticisms. She had singled out these two as royals that she especially liked and applauded for modernising the monarchy.

Julie's passionately patriotic sentiment was echoed in all the focus groups and interviews. The party leaders at the last election were judged against this criteria, and Jeremy Corbyn was found wanting. His lack of patriotism made some quite angry. Julie bristled when I asked her about him. 'He's a very arrogant man,' she said. 'He doesn't listen and he cares more for Britain's enemies than he does for Britain. He doesn't think of them as terrorists, he thinks of them as victims. He'd quite happily have got more people in, reduced the army and made us vulnerable.' She shudders to think what this might have mean if he had been Prime Minister. Jenny Chapman, the former Labour MP for Darlington, had heard similar complaints on the doorstep again and again: 'There's almost nothing new to say here. At every other door it was, "We can't vote for you while he's the leader – he's a terrorist. He'll betray us."' Gareth Snell, the former Stoke-on-Trent MP, echoed this too: 'We had stopped talking to people about the things they cared about. They thought Jeremy Corbyn was more interested in what was happening in far-flung corners of the world than about what was going on in Britain.' By contrast, Boris Johnson fared well with many voters by talking about his love of the country. Julie said, 'Of course he's patriotic, he obviously thinks a lot of Britain,' while Mick, not the biggest Johnson fan, observed that 'whatever you think of him, country comes first with him. You have to give him that.' Peter Gibson, the new MP for Darlington, made a similar point: 'Boris comes across as someone who is quite happy to hold a Union Jack and I think that's been quite important.'

7

CLASS IDENTITY AND BELONGING

'I'm working class like everyone here, not middle class,
though I did vote Tory this time.'

When I begin a focus group, I always start by going round the room and asking the eight or so participants to tell me a bit about themselves by way of introduction. This is intended to be a warm-up to the conversation that follows, rather than part of the data gathering. As such, people can choose to tell me whatever they want. Mostly people offer their name, maybe their age, and where they work or what they do. They may also tell me something about their families: kids, grandkids, pets (dog people often share their beloved pet's name and breed, cat people boast about how many cats they have). Occasionally, I'm told something about their hobbies (which football team they support, what kind of cookery they favour, about volunteering activities like running a Brownie pack or helping in the local charity shop). In the Red Wall focus groups, I was fascinated by how many people, with absolutely no prompting at all from me, chose to volunteer their social class. This was both very unusual and also very revealing: clearly, being working class is a vital part of many Red Wallers' identity.

When we first set up BritainThinks, co-founders Viki Cooke, Ben Shimshon and I decided to conduct a piece of work exploring attitudes to social class in Britain. We began in early 2011 with a study that considered what it meant to be middle class, and then followed up some months later looking at what it meant to be working class. We found that, back then, almost seven out of ten people self-identified as middle class. We asked those who did so to come along to focus groups bringing something that symbolised their 'middle classness'. I was astonished in the first session, held in a pleasant suburb of Leeds, when five out of eight produced cafetieres out of their bags (and one other, who did not drink coffee, brought 'posh' Twinings Earl Grey tea bags). It seemed that making a discerning choice about the beverage you liked was a better indicator than, say, home ownership – one woman had brought keys to the flat that she and her fiancé had recently bought, to be told by other group members, 'Good for you – but you really don't need to own your own home to be middle class.'

Conducting similar focus groups with people who self-defined as working class produced a very different outcome. A few months later, in May 2011, I sat in a leisure centre in Pitsea in Essex and watched as people showed each other the objects they had brought along. They had all chosen the tools of their trade as symbols of their class: a joiner had brought his toolkit, a woman who worked as a beautician had brought her acrylic nail colour swatches, while another, a hairdresser, had brought along a rather swish pack of scissors. One man delved into his rucksack to find his muddy working boots, which he pulled out and, after carefully laying down a sheet of newspaper brought along for the purpose, placed them on the table in front of him.

Being middle class had been about being discerning: knowing the difference between ground coffee and instant coffee, or classy tea and ordinary PG Tips, while being working class was about the kind of work that you do – typically, work with your hands. As one of the men in the Pitsea focus group put it, this is 'because working-class people are the ones who do all the work. You don't see a middle-class person by the side of the road fixing pipes, do you?'

Listening to Red Wall voters talk about social class – with the conversation generally revolving around their own working-class status – I was struck by the intensity of their sense of belonging to that class. If anything, it was even stronger than the sentiments I had heard expressed back in 2011. None of the Red Wallers that I spoke to were employed in traditional manufacturing industries any longer, although most were manual workers, with the men typically working in construction. Some were now working in what was described by people in Darlington as the 'service sector' – banking, retail or call centres. Others were in the 'public sector': local government or health, often caring roles which most of the women, in every location I visited, seemed to do. Despite Red Wallers' nostalgia for their area's traditional manufacturing base, working in a very different way did not seem to diminish their sense of being working class. Their social class is still the key to their identity and a badge of pride. It is about their roots, their family background and their heritage: 'I come from working-class stock.' It is about their place: 'Most people round here are working class. You've got the pit villages, as they used to call them – working class to their core.' And it is about their values and beliefs: 'It's an attitude to life – it means you want to make society more equal, be more people-focused.'

But being working class, it turned out, is not just about how you feel about yourself; it is also about how others see you. Here, many looked back to a more positive past, where the work that people like them did had dignity and commanded real respect. 'It was tough,' Gordon from Hyndburn commented: 'Long hours, hard work, dangerous work, but you were often doing something important and you were valued – and well paid for it too.' Our Red Wallers were at their most nostalgic when they talked about the 'work' part of being working class. Back then, they believed, there was the promise of a positive future, more opportunity and decent training with good apprenticeships: 'When I left school, I was offered three apprenticeships with three different firms and I could take my pick. We all could,' Bob from Darlington had told me proudly. As a worker back then you had clout. That meant better job security and pay. The trade unions were all-powerful – sometimes even too powerful. Darlington-based ex-miner Derek explained, 'You were brought up from the pit and you were told how you were going to vote in an industrial dispute. One out, all out. If they wanted industrial action you had to go along with it. My lot voted 75 per cent not to strike but we couldn't cross a picket line – it was ingrained into you.' All this seems a far cry from the 2020 workplace with zero-hour contracts and poor-quality or non-existent training.

Although working conditions have changed, most Red Wallers pride themselves on their own hard work. That sense of pride is coupled with an eagerness to distance themselves from a group about whom they were scornful: people who do not want to work. Steve, a taxi driver from Darlington, put it like this: 'We're the working class because we work – and they are not, because they don't have any intention of working.' The clue is in the name. Included in this bracket would be benefits cheats, single mums on benefits and some – though crucially not all – immigrants. This was a hot topic in the Red Wall: if there is one thing worse than immigrants who come over to the UK and undercut British workers' wages, it is immigrants coming to the UK with no intention of working at all. Almost everybody I spoke to was able to provide examples from their own neighbourhood. Sometimes this was 'home-grown', as with Michelle from Accrington's irritation at the single mums at the bottom of her road getting free accommodation and 'welfare hand-outs'. However, the fiercest criticism was reserved for people many believed to have come to the UK with the specific objective of taking advantage of British welfare. Maureen from Darlington's fury at 'being overrun by immigrants on the take, claiming benefits and sending them home' was typical and I heard many comments that 'we are mugs', or that Britain is a 'soft touch', with ordinary working-class people apparently being 'taken for fools'.

Being working class is not just about who you are or how others perceive you. It is also about what you are *not*. For many of the Red Wallers I met, it probably meant *not* being a graduate. Many challenged the notion that university is a guaranteed route to a successful career for youngsters and were concerned about young people being encouraged to take on massive debt to obtain what they see as 'worthless' degrees. Mick pointed out that jobs for people with degrees in Darlington are few and far between: 'If you want to be a graduate trainee then you probably need to go to Newcastle or Manchester.' Meanwhile Bob felt that there should be more career planning. He reckoned it should be compulsory for young people to make a career plan and develop a sense of where they want to be in ten years' time: 'Then they could decide if going to uni is right for them or if it's just going to be an expensive waste of time. They shouldn't do it until they've set out their own goals. Otherwise they're just accruing debt at the rate of £50,000 a head.'

Several of the men worried that being a graduate didn't usually qualify you to do anything much anyway. 'It's alright if you want to be a doctor or a lawyer – then sure, go to uni – but if you want to be in business, then it's better to get work experience. The university of life!' noted Jeff, himself an HGV driver. He felt that learning on the job, especially with the kind of old-fashioned apprenticeship many of them had done themselves, was a more useful undertaking: 'I did day release for years and it was brilliant.' Jo Gideon, the incoming

Conservative MP in Stoke-on-Trent, had quickly identified apprenticeships as an important area to campaign for and develop in her new constituency.

To some, having a degree seemed like another, modern-day version of 'them and us', a world in which people who were graduates give themselves unwarranted airs and graces. There was often an inverse snobbery to this sentiment. Yvonne, the local activist who had fought so hard and so successfully to save Darlington Library, described herself as 'one of the little people', and in conversation talked constantly about being 'self-educated'. In part, this explained her passion for libraries and their ability to open up learning opportunities to everyone, but she also spoke with an air of defiance. She clearly believed that graduates wrongly considered themselves to be superior. She almost dared those people with their fancy degrees to look down on her: 'They don't listen to the likes of us. They think they know best – I mean they think they know what's best for us.'

Despite all this, nothing made the people I met more proud than their own children going to uni – usually being the first member of their family ever to do so. Bob told me about his younger son, who he had long believed might go to uni: 'From fourteen or so, I knew he had it in him.' Initially, though, Bob had been alarmed that the boy was very taken with drama and started talking about going to drama school. Of this, Bob took a dim view, rolling his eyes to heaven as he tells his story: 'You don't want to burst their bubble, but I asked him, what's your Plan B? Drama's all very well, but what if it doesn't work out?'

Bob was both delighted and relieved when work experience arranged by the school found his son helping out as a teaching assistant and loving it. 'He then said to me that he'd rather be a teacher than an actor, and he went to Gloucestershire uni, which is very good for teaching, and now he's a teacher and loving it.' Bob glowed with pride as he told me about visiting his son, currently teaching in a school in Italy. He added that he now thought that his son would probably consider himself middle class...

This created a sense of social mobility for some, which played out in interesting ways when we look at the impact of class on votes. Many of the people I spoke to felt that they had changed and their lives were very different from those of their parents and grandparents – and they hoped that their children's lives would be different again. Bob told me, 'We're more affluent now, we have more disposable income, but we have more to pay for and more to do with the money.' Malcolm explained that his miner father had just two modes: 'He was either in bed waiting to go to work, or at work just slogging away exhausted and ready to get back to bed.' Back in 2011, the BritainThinks class study showed that although there was already some disillusionment with Labour, it was still the party of choice for those who self-defined as working class. That said, again and again I heard a nostalgia for the Labour of the past, a Labour that was intimately connected to their working-class status. This was echoed and amplified in 2020 when I asked Red Wall voters if Labour – the Labour they left because it had disappointed them – had ever been what they had wanted it to be. The answer was always firmly in the past: 'Years ago they were good – when I was coming up to voting age my mum said to me, "Vote Labour, your dad's a miner and Labour are for the working class,"' explained Mick from Darlington. 'Labour is the party of the working man.' This wasn't something you argued with – it was just accepted. But Labour is different now. Still, for many, the switch to Conservative wasn't done lightly: 'It's going against your whole family,' said Ronnie, the Stoke-on-Trent bus driver.

Many argue that the biggest change was not what had happened to them, but what has happened to the Labour Party, and it had been a long time coming. While some of the people I spoke to had admired Tony Blair ('Last decent leader that they had. I really liked him at first, he seemed different'), others felt that his leadership was the beginning of an ongoing peeling off from Labour and the working classes. People I chatted to in Darlington believed they knew Blair well as his constituency, Sedgefield, is nearby. However, many felt that not only was he not from the area, but he had, as Peter Gibson had described to me, used the region and its safe seat to develop his career, with little regard for the area and its people. Views were often strongly held, with one Darlington man going as far as to suggest that Blair had only been in the Labour Party because 'the Tories wouldn't have him. If he had been able to join the Tories instead, he would have done.' There was also a sense that Labour was no longer the party for people like them but was now the party of young graduates: people like Bob's teacher son, of whom he was so very proud. Bob told me how he had argued politics with his son, who was an ardent Remainer and also a fan of Jeremy Corbyn. His son was disappointed that Labour had done so badly in the 2019 election. I wondered if Bob's son was one of the intellectually superior tribes that had so annoyed Yvonne.

Since BritainThinks' 2011 class survey, there was one significant change in the views I heard in the Red Wall that was crucial to people's voting choice in 2019: the change people saw in the Tory Party and the voters they were now striving to represent. Malcolm commented that the Tories, previously the party for the rich, are now 'the party for everyone'. Beverley from Darlington, who works in Lidl, said that the Tories had had a bad reputation, but this was in the past. Yvonne felt that her library battle was a great example of the Tories being willing to listen to local people and, crucially, willing to roll their sleeves up and get stuck in with a problem when Labour's 'great and good' had walked on by. She went on to add that Brexit was an even more powerful example of this, where Labour, with its young, middle-class graduate members, felt they knew better and refused to listen. She held Labour responsible for what she described as the 'nastiness' and 'ignorance' that had emerged through the EU referendum campaign. By contrast, the Tories accepted what the public wanted and, although they had also met internal opposition, worked hard to make the policy happen.

Yvonne described Labour as 'paternalistic', although others – like Michelle in Accrington – simply felt that Labour's young, new membership was naïve. Either way, Labour had failed to step up to the mark, and in doing so had left a vacancy with working-class voters that the Tories were able to fill. Claire Ainsley, formerly executive director at the Joseph Rowntree Foundation, has written a fascinating book defining what she describes as *The New Working Class*. Her final chapter is called 'How to Win Hearts, Minds and Votes'. She highlights the importance of community and family as 'the bedrock of British values'; of 'fairness' (under this heading she argues for a 'points-based system for migration'), hard work and decency. Significantly, Ainsley is just starting a new role – as policy director for the new Labour leader, Keir Starmer.

PART TWO

WHERE DOES POLITICS FIT IN?

8

WHERE DOES POLITICS FIT IN?

'I don't trust any of them. They have no idea how we live.
And they don't care.'

In decades of studying voter response to party politics, one striking observation has always overshadowed everything else: how very little of our politicians' efforts get noticed. Busy as voters are, getting on with their own lives, those agonised-over initiatives, carefully crafted words and hours of media training all too frequently pass them by. Lord Ashcroft's polling in the 2019 election showed week after week that one in four of us remembered nothing at all from the campaign. I have often wondered how to break it gently to a senior politician that there is probably no need to be worried about skewing the findings by being recognised when observing a focus group. During the 2019 election I ran a live focus group on Victoria Derbyshire's morning TV show. In a sequence that would probably have been edited out of a pre-recorded session, one participant told us how much she liked Nigel Farage, but then went on to say that she didn't think she'd vote for him because she didn't think his party, the Lib Dems, stood for anything much. It is rare for anyone to be able to name any member of either front bench, and I recall one session where almost half the group couldn't name the then PM, David Cameron. Just a quarter say they can name their own MP and, given that this isn't often put to the test in polls, it might be reasonable to assume the actual number is somewhat lower.

The Hansard Society runs a regular poll tracking political engagement, last published in early 2019. That edition highlighted the bleakest levels of public disillusionment and disengagement in the fifteen years the survey has run. Almost every measure represented a new low. Two-thirds felt that our system of governing needed 'quite a lot' or 'a great deal' of improvement – with those saying 'a great deal' rising eight points to 37 per cent in the past year. Half believed that political parties and politicians 'don't care about people like me'. Trust in politicians has never been high but Ipsos MORI's Veracity Index a month before the 2019 election recorded the sharpest decline. Only 14 per cent said they trusted politicians – now beating much-derided advertising executives into the bottom place – with a five-percentage-point fall year on year. Furthermore, 47 per cent – another worst ever in the Hansard Society poll – felt that they have 'no influence at all' on decision-making. Fewer people agreed that their own involvement can make a difference. Unsurprisingly, this has a knock-on effect on the number of people who are politically active. Hansard has been tracking a list of possible points of engagement between the public and politics. These range from simply whether or not you vote, to getting in touch with your MP or 'contributing to the debate online'. It was found that 22 per cent are now doing 'none of the above'. Some 30 per cent said they never talked about politics or government, 26 per cent said they were not interested at all and two out of ten quite frankly admitted knowing 'nothing at all'.

This is all played out vividly in focus groups where people's frustrations with the political classes are matched only by their feelings of impotence to bring about change. Everywhere I went people talked fluently about the problems the country faces, the problems their area faces and the problems they and their family and friends face. Yet when I asked who might be able to fix things, conversation almost always ground to an abrupt halt. Even Sue from Darlington, bubbly and chatty, overflowing with ideas and opinions ranging from high street regeneration to youth clubs, faltered: 'I don't really know what's going on in politics – I don't follow things closely.' 'There's no point,' Jackie, a member of the Hyndburn focus group told me, 'They have no idea how we live.' Tracey, sitting next to her, had an idea about how to sort this: 'They should be made to live our lives. To know what it's like juggling work and kids and trying to make ends meet.' Tracey manages two jobs caring for adults with learning disabilities as well as caring for her own grandchildren and for an elderly parent. BritainThinks' 2019 Mood of the Nation study found that just 6 per cent agree that UK politicians 'understand people like me'. A staggering 73 per cent were sure that they did not.

The trigger for this book was a national political upset: Labour's Red Wall turning blue. However, the more I explored voters' feelings in the constituencies I visited, the more convinced I became that local government, so often overlooked by politicians and commentators operating at a national level, matters much more in constituencies like those in the Red Wall. If a group of voters have long felt neglected and ignored by national government, then what happens locally takes on a greater importance. This is particularly true when people's lives are contained within the area they come from; place means more when you live, work and socialise nearby. The most immediate evidence of how political parties perform is seen through the lens of local government: are they on my side? Do they spend my money wisely? Are their priorities my priorities? Do I admire their leadership? This does not necessarily mean that people will engage more in local democracy – turnout in Hyndburn in 2019's local elections was a poor 31 per cent – but if this is how voters are judging the parties, it can also be a useful predictor of how they might behave in a national contest.

Listening to Red Wall voters, I was reminded of a project in Scotland ahead of the 2012 local elections. I had been approached by Labour MPs Margaret Curran and Anas Sarwar on behalf of Johann Lamont, the then Scottish Labour leader. At the time, Glasgow was under 'no overall control' – effectively a hung council – and there was concern in the Labour camp that the SNP might actually win the city that Labour regarded as its own. I conducted focus groups with long-standing Labour voters who were considering voting SNP. The findings took me aback. I had rarely heard such fury in focus groups. Frankly, voters were spitting with rage. They felt angry and neglected. They believed that the Labour government had let them down, and spoke of the north–south divide, meaning that resources and investment never found their way up to Scotland. They felt that their votes, crucial to past Labour victories, had not been properly earned for years. They felt taken for granted. They told me that Labour had used Scotland as a sort of political academy for its brightest and best, who then headed south to further their careers in Westminster, never looking back. Gordon Brown, Alistair Darling, Robin Cook and many more stood accused of this. I spent a miserable afternoon debriefing a very bad-tempered Johann Lamont on these findings. She pushed back and challenged me on every point. In the event, Labour survived in Glasgow a few months later, regaining control of the local council. But the findings foretold the rout that was to come in the general election of 2015, in which Labour lost all but one of Scotland's fifty-nine seats, most of which it had held for decades. It was a catastrophic electoral impact from which Labour has still not recovered.

I heard many of the same themes – entitlement, neglect and lack of empathy – expressed again and again in the Red Wall. Peter Gibson, the new Conservative MP for Darlington, used almost exactly the same language as the Glaswegian voters when talking about Labour in the north-east. The area had been, he claimed, 'used as a training ground' for the Labour 'great and good'. Promising politicians cut their political teeth in seats like Sedgefield (Blair), Darlington (Milburn), Hartle-pool (Mandelson) and South Shields (David Miliband). These seats were particularly attractive, Gibson believed, because they barely required the MP to be there, so safe were they thought to be. It was a similar story in Stoke-on-Trent. No one could name Tristram Hunt, glamorous historian, Labour MP since 2010 and shadow Education Secretary, until he stepped down to become director of the V&A museum, causing the by-election that Gareth Snell won in 2017. The area was there-fore doubly neglected: first by national government and then again by their local MP, typically an outsider who barely took the trouble to be there and never got to know the area or its people, retreating to London and London ways as soon as pos-sible. The almost certainly apocryphal story that did the rounds when Peter Mandelson was MP for Hartlepool summed this up well: ordering lunch in a local fish-and-chip shop, Mandel-son allegedly spotted a bowl of mushy peas: 'I'll have cod and chips, please – oh, and some of your delicious-looking avocado dip on the side.'

When I asked Red Wallers who could make a difference to them locally, many talked – for good or bad – about the local council before they talked about national government, although there was often confusion about who is responsible for what and about which party is in control. In Stoke-on-Trent, focus group members assumed the council is still Labour, although Labour had lost control some time before and the current leader, Abi Brown, is a Conservative. Some voters in Accrington thought that the council had changed hands and was Tory-controlled because the area now had a Tory MP. (Given Hyndburn Council's somewhat negative reputation, this is a myth Labour might wish to perpetuate.) Most, however, knew that it is a Labour council – a Labour council that got it in the neck for many of the problems that people identified in the local area: the run-down town centre; dirty, neglected streets; failure to get to grips with the local drugs problem; lack of youth services; and poor-quality roads – 'pot holes everywhere'. In many voters' minds, these things sum up Labour's shortcomings and anticipate the chaos that Labour might wreak if it were to win control of the national levers of government and, worse still, the purse strings.

Graham Jones, the outgoing Labour MP in Hyndburn, was very clear when I asked him if he would, with hindsight, have done anything differently. The council came up straight away:

> District councils can become inward-looking, especially when they have to make deep cuts. I suspect the Conservatives had hard constituency analysis that told them that, after the Labour leader and Brexit, the third issue that the Tory candidate should put on her leaflets and speak out about was dissatisfaction with Hyndburn Council – which is exactly what Sara did time and time again.

He was regretful about Hyndburn Council's negative reputation, not least because he believes people treated it as a 'yardstick' for how a national government of the same political hue would fare. Michelle told me that the council's preoccupation with bureaucratic rules and regulations, which she as a local business owner had to stick to, indicated their lack of under- standing of what makes a successful business, as well as their tendency to waste money – her money. She was furious about how high the business rates were and had resolved to go to the next council meeting. 'It's an open meeting – anyone can go – and I'm going to go along,' she told me defiantly. 'I'm going to check where all my money goes.' She was also irritated that 'others' – by this she meant local business owners from BAME backgrounds, which she spelt out in no uncertain terms – in her view got away with far less regulation than she had to grap- ple with. She repeated her anecdote about a local corner shop where mice are 'running all over the counters' and no one puts a stop to it.

Most of the reactions to local councils that I heard were uni- formly negative. Everywhere I went, participants shared a view that funds are not distributed fairly. There tended to be huge resentment about the allocation of council houses and a belief that less deserving people knew how to 'play the system': young women deliberately becoming pregnant by multiple fathers; drug addicts and dealers (in every constituency I visited voters complained about substance abuse, a fairly new and now major issue); or the 'professional poor'. There were many stories about each of these. The Accrington women swapped stories about a man who has a slot begging outside the local Tesco, who can be spotted disappearing off in a rather smart car at the end of his shift: 'His car is a lot nicer than mine,' complained one. Julie, a cleaner from Darlington, told me how she felt treated like a 'second-class citizen in my own country'. Her grievance, like Michelle's, was partly about political correctness that she felt the council, when Labour, had enthusiastically embraced: 'You have to watch your Ps and Qs. They don't like you putting flags out and they don't like you celebrating Christmas.'

Another complaint about the local council was how well or badly it managed the local town centre. Accrington was felt to be in serious decline and, it seems to me, the local council can't win. Popular moves, like the recent refurbishment of the market and the Town Hall square, were taken for granted, with a shrug that 'of course, they should do that', it's a basic requirement. Meanwhile, holes were picked in many other initiatives: the sparkling new bus station is in the wrong place ('Too far from Tesco') and the 'cornflake' resurfacing of the Arndale Centre approach is thought both costly and ugly. The council was also blamed for decisions about which it probably had little agency, such as the local M&S closure. Most of all, though, there was concern about misplaced priorities and unfairness in allocating funds, such as helping drug users rather than helping them and their families. To many Red Wallers, all this implies misplaced priorities, often driven by a political correctness that sees locals like them fall far down the pecking order.

It's a similar story in Stoke-on-Trent, where the council was harshly criticised for its profligacy, apparently installing very expensive granite benches, which brickie Colin pointed out 'no one ever sits on – apart from winos and beggars', throughout the town. Despite Hansard's findings about dwindling levels of political engagement, several claimed that they would like to have been consulted on some of the decisions taken, and it did seem to me that involving ordinary members of the public in some of the decision-making might have been an effective way to counter the ill feeling and get the public on board.

Darlington citizens were on the whole happier with their town centre, but the previous Labour council had earned a big black mark for its proposed library closure. It had become, in the eyes of some like Yvonne Richardson, a symbol of the council's failure to listen to local people until their votes, taken for granted for so long, looked to be in jeopardy.

Once in a while, though, a local politician manages to cut through and get noticed, acting as a positive ambassador for the party that he or she represents. Ben Houchen, Tory mayor for Tees Valley since 2017, is a rare example of this, giving lifelong Labour voters in Darlington and other constituencies in the area the licence to consider his party as a positive option. Newly elected Tory MP for Darlington Peter Gibson has already begun working very closely with Houchen, clearly hoping that by doing so a little of the magic will rub off. Gibson proudly told me about Houchen's project to buy back the airport: 'It felt almost like a fantasy at the start of the campaign, but against the odds he did it. Now he's known as the Ronseal politician locally. Incredibly popular. He's from here, like me. He's about pragmatic politics. He's a straight talker. Grew up here and belongs here.' Gibson credits Houchen with laying the ground for the Tories, not just for winning Darlington but also Redcar, Cleveland, Middlesbrough and Hartlepool.

For many of the people I met, the one electoral moment

that stood out as different from business as usual was Brexit. Though often not mentioned at first, it would surface at some point and was often seen – including by those who had voted Remain – as an antidote to the wrongs they had identified with all politics, local, national and international: 'It'll shake things up – and goodness knows we need that.' BritainThinks' Brexit Diaries project found that 90 per cent of Leavers and 84 per cent of Conservative voters believed exactly that: 'Brexit has given the political establishment the shake-up that it urgently needed.' But more than that, Brexit was expected to be a panacea to so many of the wrongs that voters see around them. Retired butcher Ken told me that, for the first time, he now felt optimistic about his grandkids' future: 'We used to have the best of engineering, agriculture and fisheries. And now that we can set our own rules, we will again.' He lamented the loss of manufacturing: 'This area used to be known for its weaving sheds and now there aren't any at all.' I asked him, 'Was this the EU's fault?' He was unsure, but he did feel that Brexit represented the new start the country needed, and that was enough for him for now.

The optimism that Ken expressed was widespread. Michelle believed that the country would be strong again – and independent. She told me that 'being independent would lead to more jobs, especially if we only allowed in immigrants with the skills we need, like doctors'. Michelle's bigger goal was echoed by most people I spoke to: to use the act of leaving Europe to revitalise our manufacturing industry and bring back jobs. She also thought it would allow us to rebuild our agriculture, asking me if I knew where my milk came from. 'Where?' I asked. 'Holland,' she announced. 'Holland – when it's not as if we don't have cows round here!' And that, she thought, was about to change at last.

9

BREXIT

'The sun is shining in a blue sky on the morning of
February 1st 2020. I take that as a stamp of approval
and a pat on the back by the universe.'

Despite Red Wallers' disillusionment with politics, Brexit stood out as the one vote they really believed might make a difference. Almost all of the Red Wall constituencies voted Leave. Most, though not all, of the people I interviewed there had been Leave voters, and those who were not tended to believe that we should now put Brexit behind us and 'move on'. It was clear that they regarded what they saw as Labour's intransigence on this topic as further evidence of it not being the party that stood up for them any more. If Labour had been a Remain party, it had failed miserably to make its case to Red Wallers, choosing instead to wobble precariously on the fence and ending up pleasing no one. Whatever they had voted, most Red Wallers felt that their views had been disregarded, particularly their overwhelming eagerness for an end to the Brexit stalemate. None had any appetite at all for another referendum, and even suggesting one seemed an affront to the popular view that 'the people had spoken'.

At BritainThinks, we had been tracking voters' perceptions of Brexit throughout the referendum campaign, and then during the Brexit process, with our 'Brexit Diaries' project. Immediately after the referendum, our polling was startling in its depiction of a divided country where 56 per cent described themselves as 'have-nots'. This average became more pronounced when we took geography into consideration: 77 per cent in the north-east identified as 'have-nots', as did 62 per cent of Leave voters, compared with only 49 per cent of Remainers. We found that this division was in part explained by people's underlying attitudes. The 'have-nots' believed that the country had long been run in the interest of a small group of 'elites', who at best had no understanding of the difficulties they faced in their day-to-day lives, and at worst didn't actually care: 'They're the big people. They think that we're a united country because they don't know anything about our lives.'

Brexit was not the cause of this malaise, but it had now brought those simmering divisions to a head. In a focus group in Harlow a couple of weeks after the vote, one man described waking up and learning that we'd 'gone Brexit'. He felt as if 'England had won the World Cup' and described running round his bedroom punching the air with joy. He also told me how much he had enjoyed 'sticking two fingers up to "them"'. I asked who he meant by 'them'. 'The elites,' he told me. He was referring to the same 'elites' that had made Yvonne Richardson so angry: 'I started being for Brexit but then there was all the nastiness. They started attacking people like me and calling us ignorant and ill-educated. It was paternalism: we know best. I was so upset and angry and hurt about that.'

BritainThinks' first Brexit Diaries wave kicked off in early 2017, immediately after Article 50, the legal mechanism by which a member state leaves the EU, was triggered. We identified four Brexit 'tribes'. First, the 'Die Hards', voters who, like the Harlow focus group member, were totally delighted by the referendum result. Also Leave-voting but with some reservations about what the future might hold were the next group, whom we described as the 'Cautious Optimists'. On the Remain side we found 'Accepting Pragmatists', who had voted Remain but now, reluctantly, felt that maybe it would be better if we did leave. And finally there were the 'Devastated Pessimists', whom we illustrated with an icon of a man with his head on his desk in despair. These were Remain voters who could see no possible positive outcome from leaving the EU. While many of the people I met in the Red Wall represented the Die Hard group, the Devastated Pessimists included many of the 'elites' that had so antagonised both Yvonne Richardson and the Harlow man.

At the outset, we found significant polarisation, with the population clustering into the two more 'extreme' groups: Die Hards and Devastated Pessimists represented around a third of the population each, with the remaining third made up by combining the two middling, 'swing voter' groups. Tracking attitudes over time, the most interesting observation turned out to be how little things changed. While each side claimed victory at various points throughout the Brexit process, in reality those groups remained pretty consistent in size right up to our final wave, published after the Withdrawal Bill finally passed at the end of January 2020.

During this time, the BritainThinks project revealed some fascinating attitudinal differences between the groups. We began with a diary exercise, where voters were asked to keep diaries over time, noting whatever struck them as important as the Brexit process got going. We learned that, while Remain voters were pretty preoccupied with the economic impact of leaving the EU, noticing stories about international investors withdrawing funds, factory closures and job losses, this was something that Leavers barely thought about. Left to comment on whatever they wanted, free of prompts from us where asking a question can risk framing the answer, most Leavers' observations related to stories they had read and the conversations they were having about sovereignty and independence; freeing ourselves from EU rules and regulations; and ending the dominance of 'politically correct' elites in Europe and the UK. Paula Surridge, psephologist at Bristol University, has conducted interesting analysis of the role that voters' values play in their voting decisions. She has developed a scale which she describes as 'liberal–authoritarian', driven by views on questions including belief in the death penalty, in stiffer prison sentences and in censorship. Many Leavers sat firmly at the 'authoritarian' end of this axis.

However, as events unfolded, and after Theresa May's disastrous election campaign in 2017, the two groups did find common ground, united in their despair at how badly the process was going. The reputations of all institutions and individuals involved took a hammering, especially that of the then Prime Minister. When focus groups were asked, 'If Theresa May were a car, which car would she be?', the answers were damning. I ran focus groups on her own patch, Maidenhead. 'She'd be a Reliant Robin,' one of her own constituents observed. 'A battered old three-wheeler – barely goes but you're just surprised that she manages to drive at all.' Our polling told us eight out of ten were fed up with seeing Brexit on the TV night after night, while a staggering 64 per cent told us that Brexit was bad for their mental health (this rose to more than 70 per cent for women, who were often left bearing the brunt of Brexit-related family rows). In their diaries, Leave and Remain supporters began to choose identical language to describe the situation: it was 'chaos', 'a mess', 'broken' and the country remained 'deeply divided'.

As we entered the 2019 election campaign, the voters' moods continued to be gloomy and pessimistic. While most felt that the main objective should be to sort out the impasse, our polling told us that six out of ten doubted whether this could be achieved. However, as events unfolded, some of Boris Johnson's enthusiasm rubbed off, and almost despite themselves voters began to believe that maybe, just maybe, the impossible could happen. The single-mindedness of the Tory campaign theme paid off, confirming Tony Blair's often quoted adage that 'just when you are fed up to the back teeth of hearing a message – that's the moment when voters are just starting to hear it'.

BritainThinks ran a large workshop with some fifty undecided voters for the BBC in Crewe on the Monday before polling day. We asked them to shout out any campaign theme that they could remember on the count of three. Without hesitation, and as one, they shouted, 'Get Brexit Done!' It was the only line that had cut through, its resonance partly a product of effective communications and partly because, for many, this was such a desirable outcome.

Typically, the Red Wall seats are different from the population as a whole, with a far greater representation of Leave groups and many fewer Devastated Pessimists, especially amongst the people who switched from Labour to Tory. Some 66.2 per cent of Hyndburn voters voted Leave, 56.2 per cent in Darlington and 69.4 per cent in Stoke-on-Trent, earning it the nickname 'Brexit Central'. Despite Leave voters' early focus on sovereignty rather than the economy, the Red Wall voters I listened to had now clearly begun to join the two up. Many of their greatest grievances were and are economic. Closing factories, a lack of jobs and a lack of opportunities for young people are at the forefront: the change they want to see. Ken, the retired butcher from Oswaldtwistle, told me that, thanks to the election outcome, he'd 'got his spark back'. He talked a lot in the interview about 'taking back control'. When I asked what it was that he thought we might take back control of in the future, he didn't hesitate: 'Manufacturing. I'd like to see employment come back … start building – they say "if you build it, they will come", don't they? We're not at the bottom yet, or near the bottom, but if we stop going down…' His views were typical of many in the belief that leaving the EU will herald a rebalancing of the UK economy with greater focus on the north, ending the 'north–south divide'.

Kenneth went on to talk about how other countries now make things more cheaply than Britain can, though when pressed he was less sure that this was the EU's fault. As a keen angler, he was also very focused on fishing: 'In time – though it will take a fair time and all that, the seas will get richer.' Julie from Darlington was convinced too: 'If we become more independent, we'll have more jobs.' I asked her why she felt this. She was clear: 'We'll be able to stop immigrants.' Though she added that we should 'keep those who have the skills we need'. I asked what they might be: 'Doctors and solicitors,' she suggested, 'professional people.' The immigration point is an interesting one. Immigration slipped down the issues of concern to be replaced by health after people felt that 'Brexit was done'. But of course, all that had actually been done was to pass the knotty problem of immigration to UK government. It remains to be seen what this government, or any future government, will do with this, but the citizens' jury that BritainThinks ran for Labour Together is clear that immigration, temporarily retired from centre stage, will remain a big issue for Red Wallers.

Julie was also of the view that the EU would very much regret losing us; it would be their loss, not ours. 'We'll become more self-sufficient,' she asserted, but without us propping them up she predicted that 'the rest of the EU will go downhill'. The final wave of our Brexit Diaries project, conducted in February 2020, suggests that this worldview is widespread amongst Leavers

– but that the Leave/Remain divide is as wide a gulf as it's ever been. BritainThinks found that 74 per cent of Die Hards agreed that 'when it comes to negotiating trade deals, most other countries need us more than we need them', while only 11 per cent of Devastated Pessimists thought the same. We found that Leavers and Remainers could look at the same evidence (for example, the fact that the UK imports goods from a particular country) and draw very different conclusions: 'Germany, they need us. We buy their stuff, like their cars,' said a Leaver, while a Remainer noted: 'Argentina, well, a lot of fruit comes from there, and a lot of meat as well. I think we probably need them, don't we?' We carried out an exercise where we asked focus groups to plot countries on a map where the x axis was 'need us more than we need them' versus 'we need them more than they need us' and the y axis was friend vs enemy. The findings were startling. Remainers placed literally every country they had been asked to categorise in the quartile that made them a 'friend' and also 'we need them more than they need us'. Leavers did the exact opposite, placing every country in the quartile that made them 'an enemy' and also saying that 'they need us more than we need them'.

We also found that how optimistic or pessimistic people felt about the year ahead to be highly contingent on their Brexit tribe. Some 86 per cent of Devastated Pessimists were true to their name and could not have felt more pessimistic about the future, while, in stark contrast, 89 per cent of Die Hards felt optimistic. We re-contacted our original diarists and asked them to note their responses the day after 'Brexit Day'. One Devastated Pessimist wrote, 'I am very, very sad about the whole situation and I worry about the future. I feel that we were stronger as part of the EU and that divides that have occurred during the whole Brexit mess will deepen further.' Compare the diary entry with this from a joyful Leaver: 'The sun is shining in a blue sky on the morning of February 1st 2020. I take that as a stamp of approval and a pat on the back by the universe.' All had been very conscious of the opportunity cost of Brexit, distracting politicians from the things that many voters really care about (the NHS, crime, housing), but this was also a source of sharp divide in terms of whether achieving Brexit would fix the problem. This division seemed to be gaping more widely rather than closing. Asked if the UK leaving the EU would mean more money for the NHS – the Leave campaign's original bold boast – a decisive 70 per cent of Die Hards believed that it would, while only 6 per cent of Devastated Pessimists felt the same, and instead were bracing themselves for things to get worse.

We found that 70 per cent of the total population, rising to 86 per cent of Devastated Pessimists, concluded Britain's division was here to stay. One commented, 'The Brexit sore will fester now, it won't go away.' Another, reflecting on conversations in his own community, added, 'A lot of people have viewpoints which are uncompromising, their views are polar opposites.' Yet there were some areas of consensus. All agreed that almost all politicians and political institutions (the House of Commons, the European Parliament, the Tory Party, the Labour Party), and most leaders, including Theresa May and Jeremy Corbyn, were collectively the architects of the disaster of the Brexit project that, from the referendum up until January

2020, had failed. Speculation about their motives varied: some had wilfully tried to deny the public's will, while others were simply incompetent. All had come out of this episode very badly indeed with reputations severely damaged. Some 57 per cent also agreed that the UK's reputation in the world had been damaged, with many describing Britain as being seen as a 'laughing stock', and talk of feeling embarrassed about the spectacle presented by the chaotic process. One voter suggested, 'America thinks we're mad and a mess...'

Yet another area of consensus was anxiety about the UK's future relationship with the US. Despite growing antagonism towards the EU, just 27 per cent – rising only up to 50 per cent of Die Hards – believed that we should prioritise getting a trade deal with the US over the EU. The very specific concerns relate almost entirely to negative feelings about Donald Trump. While most conceded that Trump and Johnson's relationship was good, the power was felt to lie entirely with the former, with Trump's volatility meaning he was not to be trusted. Another 62 per cent felt worried that Trump would take advantage of the UK in any future trade deal: 'Trump would say "UK all the way" – but at the last minute change his mind and let us down.'

Perhaps the most important area of consensus was about Britain's future. Despite the variance in optimism or pessimism, 63 per cent said Boris Johnson's Brexit deal is the start of a new era for the UK. Red Wallers felt this deeply. Bob from Darlington talked enthusiastically about it being a fresh start for the whole country. We saw the relief that many felt at the election result and the chance to 'move on'. Some 84 per cent, including 67 per cent of Devastated Pessimists, said that 'moving on' was what needed to happen as we accept the result and get on with our lives. In focus groups just ahead of the election, we created a UK version of the famous trump slogan and asked people to complete it: Make Britain ---- again. 'Normal' was the most popular response across the country. However, following the 31 January deadline, with stage one successfully completed, many Leavers upped their game, now craving 'greatness' rather than just 'normality'. As part of the BritainThinks Brexit Diaries project, we asked focus groups to come up with their own commemorative 50p coin. 'Rule Britannia' was emblazoned across many Leavers' designs.

Despite the damage that Brexit has wreaked on many political reputations, there is one politician who seemed to have emerged triumphant. Boris Johnson was careful to promise little throughout the election campaign, but the one thing voters know he did promise has, so far, been delivered. Johnson would seem to be one of the few 'Brexit winners', and while some Remainers are still cautious, believing that he has been opportunistic, with his personal success coming at the expense of the country, Leavers see him as a charismatic cheerleader for post-Brexit Britain. Expectations for the future were sky high. Curiously, many of the Red Wallers I spoke to early in 2020 now shared in the optimism whether or not they voted Leave. They believed that Johnson would indeed 'put the Great back in Great Britain' and, crucially, would do this in a way that rebalances the country and redirects power and resources towards their particular corner of it. 'It's a new start for the whole country – and a new start round here too.'

10

LEAVING LABOUR

'I've always been Labour, my parents have always been Labour, my grandparents had always been Labour...'

I asked the Red Wallers to write the first three words that sprang to mind when they thought of the Labour Party. It was the element of the focus group they most enjoyed. I had to keep stressing that this was meant to be an individual task, not a group one, so eager were they to share their thoughts. The negatives tumbled out. The less flattering the words were, the happier the author, each person trying to outdo the efforts of the other group members. Old fashioned, chaotic, in disarray, lazy, from the past, losers, broken, a mess, lost, antiquated, weak, liars, spenders. The list went on and on, consistent across locations, never, ever positive. 'I can't write it down, it's too rude,' laughed Maria, the shopworker from Stoke. I reassured her that I wouldn't be shocked: 'Oh, go on then, crap! They're just crap!'

All of the people I interviewed described themselves as life-long Labour voters, and, whether or not it had been a difficult decision to make the switch when they voted in December, most were now cheerfully reconciled to what they had done. Lord Ashcroft's post-election polling, turning the tables on Labour as he now urged them to 'smell the coffee' just as he had implored the Tories to do in 2005, confirms this. Voters believed that Labour deserved to lose – 62 per cent of the population agree with this, rising to 95 per cent of Labour-to-Tory switchers, or in other words basically all of them. He also found that, when asked to score Labour out of ten for their performance in opposition, the same switchers awarded the party a humiliating 2.3. This polling, studying voters who switched to Conservative across the country rather than just people in the Red Wall, found that the hierarchy of reasons for choosing to switch was, in descending order: Jeremy Corbyn (75 per cent); Brexit (73 per cent); lack of faith in Labour promises (62 per cent); Labour no longer represents people like me (61 per cent); and not liking Labour's policies (49 per cent). This was echoed in my research, though deeper exploration in the interviews and focus groups suggested the feeling that 'Labour no longer represents people like me' matters rather more than the above list implies. Gary, the fitness instructor from Accrington, was genuinely puzzled at what he perceived to be Labour's priorities at the 2019 election. He shook his head as he told me, 'Labour used to be our party but it doesn't get people like me any more.' This lack of connection is fundamental, an umbrella theme, an all-encompassing sentiment that, in people's minds, subsumes many of the other points.

One of the questions I set out to answer in researching this book was: 'Why did these people switch from Labour to Tory?' As I listened to more and more voters over the weeks, I found myself wondering if the question should have been: 'Why did these people vote Labour for so long?' It would have been hard to imagine voters more unimpressed by the party they had loyally stood by, often for decades. I began to ask what had made them vote Labour at all. The most common answer was simply that 'we always did'. For many against the backdrop of low interest in politics, this just wasn't something they had thought about very much. But when they did stop and think about it, they felt aggrieved: at best ignored and taken for granted, at worst taken for fools. 'They couldn't care less about the working man. They thought we'd always vote for them so they didn't need to bother,' grumbled Gary from Accrington.

I knew that disenchantment with Labour was not a recent phenomenon. I found that many interviewees who told me they were 'lifelong Labour' had actually left a while back. Some had given up on Labour as long ago as 2010. Others had dipped in and out. It didn't stop them thinking of themselves as Labour, but this was often a fond, nostalgic self-image rooted in an idealised past: the plump middle-aged man who used to play football and still considers himself 'sporty'. Lots of the people that I spoke to told me how their whole family had always been Labour: 'My parents were, my grandparents were. It was what we were.' Sue from Darlington explained it like this: 'Working-class people – and most of the north-east is that – all voted Labour. My mam brought me up to vote Labour. It's what you did. We all did.' Being Labour had been shorthand for a set of values that many Red Wallers passionately subscribed to but didn't think very hard about.

Over the decades I had heard those values expressed again and again: Labour had always been caring, compassionate, fair. But, as always, the devil was in the detail. When anyone stopped to think about what those values meant in practice, it seemed that, lately, they had become somewhat semi-detached from the party. It had been a very long time since the euphoric aftermath of the 1997 election victory when the whole country had embraced Labour – and what it stood for. I had struggled in the warm after-glow of that election, to recruit people who hadn't voted Labour to come along to focus groups. No one wanted to admit that they had not been part of the electoral victory that the whole nation seemed excited by. The new government's honeymoon had become a country-wide love-in. On reflection, there is another telling observation about Labour here: the party that had just won a stunning landslide victory were so committed to future electoral success, so eager to leave nothing to chance, that even in the immediate aftermath of their triumph they were still fretting about the people who hadn't voted for them.

In 2013, nearly three years after Labour lost and the Cameron–Clegg coalition was formed, Progress, the centre-left Labour think tank, asked me to conduct a study of target voters in what they called the 'frontline forty' seats: seats that Labour needed to win to achieve a clear victory in 2015. We visited four seats: Crewe & Nantwich, Redditch, Finchley & Golders Green and Harlow – the latter is a real weathervane seat, having gone with the winner in every election bar one since 1955. We played a 'personification game', a technique often used by commercial brands to understand their 'personality' with customers: 'If brand X were a person, what would they be like?' I tasked voters in these swing seats with imagining 'Mr or Ms Labour, the person Labour would be if the party were brought to life – and at a party. What would they chat about? What would they wear? What music would they enjoy? What would they eat and drink?' I had first tried this back in the 1980s, importing the technique from my previous day job in advertising. Then, the Labour character was always a very traditional (male) worker – a man wearing a cloth cap, eating a pie and drinking a pint; a *Mirror*-reading trade unionist living in the north of England. It is worth noting for the sake of clarity that this was not an attractive or aspirational image to would-be voters back then, but instead reflected both Labour's heritage and the reason why Labour had been out of power for so long. Changing this image to something that those voters wanted to belong to was part of the ten-year struggle to get back into power in 1997.

It turned out that, by 2013, Labour – and it was, they felt, *Mr* Labour – had become a bit of an oddball: 'He spends ages sorting through the CDs to avoid talking to the other guests,' and 'he's a bit socially awkward, listening politely but not really taking it in'. When he did join in the conversation, he 'doesn't have much to say'. He was wearing a suit that at a glance looked ordinary but on closer inspection actually seemed to be pretty expensive. His tie was brown – apparently 'he threw the red one in the bin' a while ago. His dinner had changed from a regular pie and a pint to a much more gentrified 'sausage *en croute*' accompanied by craft ale from a micro-brewery in a smart part of town, probably costing a fiver a glass. The cloth cap-wearing worker had been replaced by someone no longer authentically working class – in fact, no longer authentic at all. His identity was a muddle that few could relate to. Labour had shed its past but seemingly not replaced it with anything else. It was as if those thirteen years in government had never happened. The picture that these undecided voters painted seemed half formed. They no longer knew what Labour was about, and, they felt, neither did Labour. Asked to depict the main parties as cars, voters drew what they described as a 'clapped-out old banger on bricks' for Labour. It had a steering wheel at the front and at the back: 'They have no idea what direction they want to go in,' commented one. Later in the same session I asked, 'What is Labour's vision for Britain?' This was met with a full ten seconds of silence as everyone looked around the room to see if anyone else had any ideas. Finally, one broke the silence: 'Maybe that's just us all not paying enough attention to the news. Or maybe they don't actually have one.'

These voters would not have been very surprised when Labour went on to lose in 2015. Harriet Harman became temporary leader and commissioned me and my team to conduct an analysis of what went wrong, to feed into the party's own inquiry. We created a mood board to use in focus groups, a montage of pictures of dozens of different types of people. I showed this to the groups and asked voters who had switched from Labour to the Tories which types of people they felt would benefit from the new Conservative government. As expected, they selected people who looked like traditional Tory voters: bankers and business leaders, men in pin-striped suits sitting in boardrooms. But they also picked out people who looked a bit like them: nice-looking families with kids, ordinary young people at work or socialising, attractive older people enjoying time with their friends or grandkids, people having fun or on holiday. When I asked who would have benefited if Labour had won, almost everyone struggled. It was hard to choose anyone despite the array of more than forty images of different sorts of people in front of them. In the end they picked out the ones who looked most needy – the homeless guy, the woman in a wheelchair – or, more worryingly, most 'on the make' – Dee from Channel 4's *Benefits Street*. The voters making these choices were ordinary people: hairdressers, carers, electricians, retired delivery drivers and receptionists. Their main point was that, whoever might have benefited from a Labour government, it certainly wasn't people like them.

Against this backdrop, it's not hard to see the appeal that Jeremy Corbyn held for many party members. More of the same did not seem like a good option and there was a hunger – amongst the membership at least – for a decisive break with the more recent past, along with an urge to move away from the centre to a more distinctive ideological positioning. This, combined with a surge of new members determined on revolution, secured Corbyn's victory, bringing with it a radical change of direction. As the country tired of austerity, Labour set about reinventing itself. Despite the dire predictions of many commentators, me included, Labour did better than expected in the election that came two years later, robbing Theresa May of the victory she assumed was in the bag. Voters awarded Corbyn the benefit of the doubt, and attacks on him failed to land, while Theresa May proved to be a terrible campaigner.

Repeating the personification exercise in Crewe in 2018, just a year after the election, it seemed that Labour's metamorphosis was finally complete – and not in a way that would help the party with those Red Wall voters who observed that Labour was no longer even pretending to be the party of the worker. It was someone 'posh' living in a rather grand house in London and eating fancy food: quinoa was the most frequent suggestion. Those Crewe voters could not have been more scornful. They had nothing in common with this version of Labour; it was a Labour Party that had no understanding of how they lived their lives. I spoke to Paula Surridge, the respected academic from Bristol University who has been analysing party identity by values. I asked her why Labour lost in 2019 and she was very clear in her answer: the 2019 defeat had been coming for a while…

Labour moved away from these voters, not the other way round. Labour just didn't do much for them. This had started while Labour was in government and afterwards, rightly or wrongly, there was the sense that Labour hadn't delivered much. But then, after 2010 Labour seemed to focus on things that were not their agenda. And that feeling was turbo-charged after Jeremy Corbyn became leader.

Red Wall voters in 2020 agreed with this verdict. Labour was the party for 'the south'. When asked who would have been the winners had Labour won, the response was similar to that back in 2015, although there was a new addition. As before, they told me that 'Labour was the party of losers and scroungers', but now Labour was also the party of 'naïve and idealistic middle-class students' – arrogant kids boasting degrees but lacking life experience, young people who looked down on people like them. Several focus group members were aware of the dramatic increase in the party's membership and believed that there had been some kind of take-over bid by self-serving activists who held extreme views and saw the world in a very different way from the Red Wallers. Yvonne Richardson described it to me: 'Older people can see the bigger picture, but the younger people see themselves as educated – but they've only got that much vision', she gestured a tiny gap between her fingers. 'They think they're educated because they've got a degree. Tribes running Labour who think they know better than everyone and think people like me are ignorant. How dare they?'

Lord Ashcroft's research highlights this gulf between party members and voters. His February 2020 research shows a revealing difference between the views of disaffected past Labour voters and those of Labour members. The latter believe that Labour lost because the media represented Jeremy Corbyn unfairly. They were concerned that voters believed Tory 'lies' and thus didn't understand what a Tory vote would mean. Agreeing that 'many voters have bigoted views about race and immigration that the Tories were able to exploit', they confirmed

Red Wall voters' fears that Labour judged rather than understood its previously loyal base. Meanwhile, those voters who abandoned Labour saw it quite differently, saying that Jeremy Corbyn was not 'an appealing leader'; that Labour was divided, with election promises that were not credible; and, crucially, that Labour 'no longer really represents its traditional voters'.

One example of this was the trans debate, which was dominating the leadership contest when I was up in Accrington in March 2020. The men were genuinely baffled about this. 'How many trans people are there?' one asked the others in the focus group. No one knew, but they all decided that it must be a very small group as they had never met anyone who matched that description. Gary was exasperated: 'There's thousands of kids here with no work and no hope. Why don't they think about them instead?'

There's another echo from the past here. Back in the late 1980s, when I was first asking focus groups to personify the Labour brand, another stereotype emerged sitting oddly alongside the cloth-capped trade unionist factory worker. This was a London-specific persona that emerged out of what the tabloid media back then dubbed the 'loony left'. Focus group members in marginal seats around the country had a clear image of this character as someone who was 'bonkers', 'militant', wearing 'dirty, hippy clothes', living 'in a squat'. It was someone who liked to 'smoke pot' and was pretty 'weird' – and, of course, a 'loony'. Supporting the CND (Campaign for Nuclear Disarmament) was the policy that most vividly conjured up the preoccupation of this group. Needless to say, the target voters did not share this policy priority.

This version of Labour, politically correct, morally superior and fixated on the wrong priorities was, if anything, even more alienating to Red Wallers in 2020 than it had been to swing voters ahead of the '87 election. For some, the Labour Party activists just seemed out of touch and naïve, but for others there was a more sinister note. The outputs from their personification game could not have been less attractive. If the Labour Party of the December 2019 election campaign were to come to life it would embody all the very worst attributes of the generic politician: greedy, selfish, hypocritical and also incompetent. Labour was bitterly condemned for its 'for the poor' positioning. People in Accrington felt that meant the party was somehow riding on the back of the poor, using them for its own political gain: 'Keeping the poor poor,' one said. 'Keeping everyone down and dependent on them.' Crucially, as Tracey, a care worker from Accrington, commented, 'For the poor but not for the poorly paid like us.'

Ashcroft's poll illustrates this well. Just 5 per cent of Labour-to-Tory switchers said that Labour's values were close to those of the British public. Even people who did vote Labour were 17 per cent less likely to be doing so for positive reasons than Tory voters, who had often made a positive choice. Some 36 per cent of Labour voters said they were mainly voting against another party rather than in favour of their own. Only half of those who did vote Labour said they 'identify' with the party, and half of Labour voters who switched to the Tories said, 'I used to identify with Labour or think of them as my party but not any more.' This reflects the verdict in Hyndburn,

Darlington and Stoke-on-Trent: Labour may have been the party of my parents and my grandparents, but it's not my party any more.

Of course, it is not just the Labour Party that is thought to have changed. Some of the voters I chatted with felt they had changed too. This was particularly true in the more affluent and upbeat Darlington. Bob was sure that he was working class, but equally sure that 'being working class isn't a prison. It doesn't define me or how I think.' Others in the men's focus group agreed. 'The world has changed and the working man has changed,' one ex-miner told me. Ronnie, a 48-year-old electrician, agreed: 'We've all moved on. We're better off than our parents could ever have dreamt of being. We wanted to get on and we did get on. How many of us now own our own home?' Most nodded round the table. Home ownership was perhaps the most potent symbol of achievement for many of the people that I spoke to. In the Darlington women's group, Sue, a shopworker, told me proudly that her daughter was 'a property owner at twenty-two'. Sue had put down the deposit out of her own savings and felt thrilled that her daughter is 'on the ladder now. Set up for life…' While voters like Sue had changed, the Labour Party seemed stuck in the past, failing to understand or respond to her aspirations.

It seems that you have to go back quite a long way to find a time when Labour was a party that Red Wallers identified with or admired. The early days of the Blair era were mentioned by a few. Back then, some felt, the Labour Party was 'aspiration-al', understanding that voters wanted to 'make something' of themselves. It was also positive and hopeful. Given that one of Labour's biggest problems is the sense that they are 'stuck in the past' (words like 'old-fashioned', 'outdated' and 'party of the past' were by far the most common in our 'three words that spring to mind' exercise), it's an irony that it is necessary to look back more than twenty years to find a time when these voters felt that Labour was the party that 'got them'. It is also an irony that the achievements of that Labour government have been written out of the party's history, eclipsed by the all-consuming negative of Iraq. While, of course, future electoral success will be contingent on Labour redefining itself for the future, it is hard to see how the party can overcome its deep-rooted negatives without some kind of rehabilitation of its most recent period in government and its most electorally successful leader ever.

11

'LOANING VOTES' TO THE TORIES

'Boris has de-snobbified the Tories...'

When I first ran focus groups for Labour, back in the 1980s, I asked a focus group in Roehampton to describe a typical Tory politician. The stereotypes were hard-wired. He – and yes, it was definitely a 'he' despite the fact that the Tory Prime Minister at the time was a woman – was 'upper class', wore a pin-striped suit, read *The Times*, drank champagne. He was confident, 'a good speaker', they told me. He probably worked in finance in the City. The astonishing thing about this stereotype is how little it changed throughout the decades that followed.

As the Labour Party was quietly morphing from 'a pie and a pint', through its 'sausage *en croute* and craft ale' phase to its Corbyn-era quinoa mode, the Tories' *Come Dine with Me* signature dinner was always the poshest food anyone could dream up: beef wellington or maybe quail, washed down with champagne or a costly vintage wine, 'Chateau something or other'. Their car of choice was likewise a Rolls-Royce or a BMW. When I ran workshops for Progress and asked them to imagine 'the party at a party', while 'Mr Labour' in 2015 was socially awkward and somewhat inauthentic, 'Mr Conservative' was garrulous, over-confident, even arrogant. He would hold forth to a bunch of identikit men in similar, very expensive, well-cut suits, before dad dancing with toe-curling enthusiasm.

Asking the same question in February 2020 confirmed how settled the Tory brand was. 'I always thought the Tories were snobby,' said Tracey, a carer from Accrington. 'Snobbish, corporate and arrogant,' said Andrew, a retired mechanic, who had lived in Hyndburn all his life. 'Self-centred, rich, privileged,' announced Jean, a healthcare worker from Stoke. Almost everyone in the group introduced themselves as the opposite of this description – they were 'working class', as had been their parents and grandparents. Gordon, a retired 'sparky', was typical: 'We were all working class: Dad were a clippy, and me mam were in catering, working in the canteen at the general hospital. Lived here most of my seventy-four year.' Unprompted, and despite my best efforts to save the politics till a later stage in the discussion, many would follow this up by going on to say how their working-class identity meant they had historically been Labour voters. As Gary explained, 'We're working class, my family and myself, and as working-class people I suppose you could say that we always used to be aligned with the Labour Party values.' All the more interesting, then, that these groups of voters were sitting drinking coffee and eating custard creams in the panelled meeting room of the Accrington Mercure hotel, waiting to tell me why they had broken the habit of a lifetime and voted Tory.

Being known as the 'snobby party' wasn't the worst of it. In October 2002, following the Tories' second, equally disastrous, defeat to Blair's New Labour, the then party chairwoman, Theresa May, put her finger on something slightly different. 'Let's not kid ourselves,' she urged. 'There's a way to go before we can return to government. There's a lot we need to do in this party of ours. Our base is too narrow, and so, occasionally, are our sympathies. You know what some people call us? The nasty party.' A year after Mrs May made her 'nasty party' speech, Michael Howard became leader of the Tory Party. His campaign in the 2005 general election was spearheaded by advertising that made slightly coy references to some of the issues that many swing voters were most worried about. The immigration ad was particularly striking: huge 48-sheet billboards declaring, 'It's not racist to impose limits on immigration.' However, while that message might have resonated at a time when Labour was apparently turning a tin ear to voter disquiet on this topic, with Michael Howard as front man, the face of the party and the campaign, it was hard to make the point without reinforcing the very 'nastiness' that Theresa May had identified.

Throughout the 2005 election campaign, I ran a series of swing voter focus groups in Watford, a three-way marginal seat, for Radio 4's *Today* programme. As part of the manifesto launch the Tories ran extravagant full-page press ads in the form of a letter from Howard, pledging an annual limit on immigration. I tested the text blind and the content was well received. However, when the author was revealed as Howard, swing voters positivity peeled away. 'I think the ad's very good. I mean it summarises how I feel. It's just a pity you've got Michael Howard's name at the bottom. He just comes across so badly, he really does,' said one female swing voter.

The unfortunate truth was that the more these voters saw of Howard, the less they liked him. Their view shifted throughout the campaign from indifference to active dislike. He was seen as remote, vain and slippery. To some, he was frankly creepy. At his hand, the potentially popular immigration message unravelled. As one focus group member told me at the time: 'They were just trying to frighten people in this country and turn people against immigration. I agree with some of the things being said. I do worry about the amount of people coming into the country, but I don't want to pick on them.' Michael Howard had come to personify the Tory Party, amplifying the negatives that Theresa May had identified three years before. In Watford, the Tories fell back into third place and the Tory Party went on to a third defeat.

After the 2005 election, Tory peer Michael Ashcroft published the first of his forensic polling studies of the electoral landscape. Entitled 'Smell the coffee: a wake-up call for the Conservative Party', this detailed report laid bare the problems that the Tories faced in returning to power. It was not a quick fix. Ashcroft concluded that the evidence suggested the Conservatives' focus on immigration may have 'actually cost them support'. His analysis is interesting with the benefit of hindsight, as it not only tells us what was happening at the time but also foretells what was to come. He noted that 50 per cent of social class AB – professional and managerial people – agreed that Britain should 'welcome all new immigrants as long as they pass strict tests to prove that they can support themselves'. He quoted journalist Mary Ann Sieghart's observations in *Times* polling, where immigration featured heavily: the Tories' vote with DEs (working-class voters) was up by 5 per cent but fell 4 per cent with ABs (professional, middle-class voters) and 8 per cent with C2s (skilled manual workers). There is irony in his conclusion to this section: 'A tough policy on immigration was likely to play best with the group that was least likely to ever vote Tory' – i.e. DEs. He noted that a Populus poll the week before had given Labour an 18 per cent lead with this group. Almost fifteen years later, in 2019, the Tories achieved a 13 per cent lead with DEs.

The Ashcroft report went on to identify many other shortcomings in the Tories' approach – all pointing to the need for a significant rethink. The Tories did have a clear lead on handling immigration, but Labour led on the NHS, education and, crucially, the economy. He found that seven out of ten felt the Tory campaign had too little to say for itself, being too focused on the other side, negative and attacking. Fewer than four in ten agreed that 'the Tory Party is making progress and is on the right track to get back in power before long', while Labour was more likely to be seen as 'competent', 'cares about ordinary people' and 'shares my values'. Ashcroft's conclusion made uncomfortable reading for the Tory Party: 'The Conservatives did not talk about the things that mattered to people in a way that showed that they understood either their anxieties or their aspirations.' He added, 'It would be a mistake to imagine that the problem is just one of presentation. The problem was not that millions of people in Britain thought the Conservative Party wasn't like them and didn't understand them: The problem was that they were right.'

This report is scattered with clues that foretell how we got from this point to the Tories' stunning victory fourteen years later. In particular, it suggests the likely appeal of a socially conservative offer to working-class voters, and hints at the unlikely possibility of creating a coalition around that if other aspects of the Conservative brand and policy, particularly the leadership, could be addressed. Both main parties have had three leaders since then. Kenneth, from Oswaldtwistle, told me that David Cameron was the first to get him looking at the Tories again ('He was young, I thought he had some good ideas'), although Theresa May was a step in the wrong direction. 'She was just the wrong person for the job. She couldn't cope. She aged before your eyes,' he said. It was Boris Johnson, though, who finally got him 'really looking and listening to the Tory Party' in a way that he would never have done before.

Even so, electoral success in 2019 was never a shoo-in. Post-election polling showed that people made their minds up later than usual: 24 per cent in the last month, 18 per cent in the last week and 16 per cent on polling day itself. But although 'don't knows' often historically translate into 'don't votes', there never seemed much doubt that people actually would turn out to vote. BritainThinks' focus groups throughout the campaign confirmed that many felt this was a crucially important vote for the country and that people felt they should 'use their vote well'. We also knew that there was anxiety about avoiding a hung parliament with the continued stasis that would bring.

The $64,000 question, then and now, is whether those votes were simply lent to the Tories to 'get Brexit done' and make a point about Labour's very poor leader. Put another way, will the Tories be able to hang on to their newly acquired Red Wall voters and hold together the fragile alliance they have forged? Peter Gibson, the new MP for Darlington, pushed back when I asked him this question: 'I just don't feel that I'm on trial and have no legitimacy being here,' he argued. 'Every election means that votes are loaned, but if the MP works hard and is consistent and engaged then people will see that.' While there is no doubt that a popular and engaged MP is important, and something that many Red Wall seats have lacked in the past, the evidence also suggests that being popular locally is not enough; success will also depend on the MP's ability to wield influence and deliver for his or her constituency. (Gibson's Labour opponent, Jenny Chapman, was clearly popular but seemed unable to make things happen. The Darlington Library was a clear example of this.) By contrast, Gibson's early success achieving funds for Darlington station in Rishi Sunak's first Budget in March 2020 may lend credibility to his 'making Darlington great' promise, though it will remain to be seen if he can still deliver in a post-coronavirus world.

However, voters clearly have an eye on what is happening at a national level too. Jenny Chapman's defeat was as much about the image and reputation of the Jeremy Corbyn's Labour Party as it was about anything she did or didn't achieve in the constituency. This, she told me, was her doorstep experience, as it was the experience of many MPs throughout the Red Wall. Graham Jones in Hyndburn told me how voters pledging their support in 2017 would wag their fingers at him as he walked back up the drive, warning, 'You make sure you get rid of him, won't you?' Gareth Snell, while acknowledging the number of times Corbyn came up as a deterrent on the doorstep, was also clear that 2005 was a turning point both for Labour and the Tories: 'We've been in decline since then and they've been picking up votes. It's not Jeremy Corbyn's fault that we lost in 2010. If he – and Brexit – were the final straws, then what were the first dozen straws?

However badly Labour did, deciding to vote for the party associated with 'posh people' and 'privilege' was not necessarily straightforward. Whatever voters made of Corbyn, Boris Johnson was, in the run-up to December 2019, also something of a divisive figure. In focus groups during the campaign, Johnson was a mercurial figure, sometimes spoilt and self-serving but also a charismatic entertainer, decisive and energetic. Many actively disliked him. One favourite focus group question is 'Would you trust this leader to look after your home when you are on holiday?' Theresa May was rumbled as an empathy-free zone in 2017 when the voters' verdict was that they'd trust her to look after their house but not their beloved pet. Asked the same question about Boris Johnson, voters laughed, 'No, of course not, he'd probably have a party and trash the place.'

In reality, voters looked at both leaders and found them wanting. Trust was an issue for all. When we asked what attributes voters most associated with either Corbyn or Johnson, we found that they shared the same unflattering top three: 'deceitful', 'out of touch' and 'dangerous'. When asked what voters recall from the campaign, 'lies' won the second highest score (after 'nothing at all'). A BritainThinks focus group of undecided voters in Peterborough a week ahead of the election found both leaders unappealing. One summed up the feeling in the room with, 'It's not about who you agree with most, it's about who you disagree with least.' Overall, Johnson was deemed less popular as PM than many of his predecessors, although he did at least start the campaign with net positive scores, unlike Corbyn, the least popular Leader of the Opposition ever. *Times* commentator Danny Finkelstein tells a story about two men running away from a fierce tiger. One stops to tie up his shoelaces. The other asks why he's bothering, saying, 'You'll never be able to out-run a tiger!' 'I don't need to,' comes the reply. 'I only need to out-run you!'

Clearly Johnson did succeed in out-running Corbyn but that was not the only ace in the Tory Party hand as it entered the election ahead in the polls. Paula Surridge told me her research suggested that the result showcased several things coming together for Red Wall voters:

Rightly or wrongly, there was a perception that actually the long Labour government didn't do much for them. At the same time there was the perfect storm of Brexit and immigration happening, so the declining community became linked with immigration in a problematic way. Immigration became a thing that could be blamed for everything and, as there seemed to be less difference between the Tories and Labour on economic left/right issues, voters began to make their minds up based on a different set of values.

She believes that the Tories were able to connect with these values, while 'Labour seemed to be shouting, "You're wrong", rather than starting from where people are and trying to understand them'.

Finally, there was the offer. Labour promised a cornucopia of goodies so extensive as to be offering people stuff that they didn't even know they wanted, such as the much mocked 'free Wi-Fi'. Labour left the perception that they had failed to set clear objectives and, more crucially, had failed to cost their programme. The Conservatives, now much better trusted on the economy, had far less to prove, but, with their streamlined manifesto and clear messaging on the NHS (more nurses) and, most of all, on Brexit, it was easier to see how they won the day. In hindsight, it seems that the clarity of the Brexit message alone might have been enough. This, and the subsequent achievement in passing the Withdrawal Bill, was seen as a positive even by the minority of Red Wallers who had voted Remain. Karen, a Remain voter from Stoke, said, 'We'd reached the point where we really did need to just get Brexit done. We'd been swimming round and round in circles.' Meanwhile

Justine, in the same Stoke focus group and also a Remainer, observed wryly, 'We'd broken enough eggs – now we had to make the omelette.'

The first three months tends to be as good as it gets for a new PM. The first focus groups and interviews that I ran for this book were all held through February and early March 2020. Boris Johnson was still in his post-euphoria, pre-delivery honeymoon period. Those new working-class voters, even if they had held their noses to vote in the first instance, now seemed to have forgotten their own discomfort and come round to Johnson, and most professed to be comfortable with their decision. After the election, BritainThinks re-interviewed undecided voters who had voted Tory and found that, despite reservations, many had concluded Johnson was the right man for the moment. He was seen to be 'focused and determined', especially in fixing the mess that the politicians on both sides of the House had caused. I also heard again and again how he was less snobbish and elitist than the Tory Party as a whole. When I queried how an Oxbridge Old Etonian could understand people from very different backgrounds, I was told that his warmth and positivity meant that he 'liked people'. His 'buffoon act' showed that he lacked self-consciousness, his spontaneity signalled that he was authentic and down to earth, even if he is posh.

The other recurring theme was about Johnson's positivity. Against a backdrop of despair about the whole political class, he seemed to radiate hope. 'He's like a light at the end of the tunnel,' said one. 'Corbyn was all gloom and doom, but Boris

deserves a chance cos he's so positive. You want to believe him.'
Back in early 2020, Red Wall voters' optimism was often vague
and lacked very specific 'asks', but that, as we'll explore in Part
Three, does not mean it lacked ambition. By the middle of
March in Darlington, voters were focused on three things: 'He's
said that he'll get Brexit done, that he'll end the north–south
divide and, now, that he'll deal with this coronavirus thing …
We'll see, but he seems pretty confident to me, and I like that in
him.' By April, in Stoke, Covid-19 dominated the conversation
and dominated and transformed expectations of the new government. While the jury was still out on this, the eagerness to
trust in the Prime Minister's hopeful demeanour was palpable.
When times are hard, it seems, people are drawn towards and
likely to choose positive messages over negative ones, being
upbeat over handwringing. It remains to be seen if this is the
triumph of hope over experience. While nobody I spoke to told
me their vote was 'on loan', it was clear that their loyalty would
need to be earned.

12

WHY LEADERSHIP MATTERS

*'He showed true leadership qualities did Boris – from the start
to the finish he stuck his neck out and didn't back down.'*

Given how little voters absorb about any political party's specific policies, it's perhaps not surprising that the leader takes on such importance. While the party 'brand' builds over time and can outlive the politicians who represent it at any given time, in many ways the leader truly is the embodiment of the party's offer. His or her personality drives party favourability, and perceptions about his or her competence are used to judge the feasibility of delivery. Voters are electing someone not just to lead them but also to lead their country and represent their interests abroad. It's a task that they take very seriously. In every election since 1979 the leader with the highest satisfaction ratings went on to win that election. It does not correlate perfectly, but the scale of the gap between the two main party leaders' ratings is indicative of the likely scale of the gap in the election result. In 1983, Margaret Thatcher enjoyed a 29 per cent lead over Michael Foot; in 1997 Tony Blair had a 19 per cent lead over John Major: both went on to win landslide victories. However, in 2017 Theresa May's lead over Jeremy Corbyn had fallen to 6 per cent and the result was a hung parliament. Last December, Boris Johnson's lead over Jeremy Corbyn was up in double figures, so you might say the writing was on the wall from the start of the campaign.

In this respect, Red Wall voters are no different from any other: their views on the party leaders are crucial in their final decision at the ballot box. I argue that the Labour Party had lost its connection with these long-standing supporters some time before Jeremy Corbyn took the helm, but it is clear that his leadership exacerbated and accelerated an already perilous situation. By contrast, positive views of Boris Johnson managed to neutralise some long-standing negative associations with the Tory Party brand. Julie from Darlington judged him to be 'funny and down to earth even though he's posh – I do like the man.' Likewise, Maria from Stoke-on-Trent saw him as a 'strong leader who cares about the country and cares about ordinary people'. This, given the very settled view that voters had of the Tory Party previously, was no mean feat. I, in common with many pollsters and commentators, had anticipated that Johnson's own background would be off-putting to voters like Maria but, as we will see, he confounded these expectations.

Before looking in detail at how the two 2019 leaders were perceived by key voters, it's worth stepping back and thinking about what people value most in a leader. At BritainThinks, this is something that we have been monitoring over the past five years, most recently in September 2019, just a little ahead of the election. We asked voters what were the most important attributes in a leader and found consistently that integrity, being decisive and being a great communicator made the top three. Examples of leaders who exhibit these qualities emerged in the focus groups. Barack Obama, the Queen and David Attenborough were the best examples of integrity. 'It's how Obama got people behind him,' explained a voter in Walsall. 'He's a good family man.' Decisiveness was owned by Winston Churchill, Putin and Alex Ferguson: 'It's about being strong in their beliefs. Not wishy-washy. They've got to know what they want because people need to have confidence in them.' When asked for examples of a great communicator, the focus groups produced now-familiar suggestions: Obama, Churchill, and Attenborough again. Communications really matter if you are going to attract followers, they agreed: 'You could have it all in your head, but without communication you're a bad leader.'

The BritainThinks survey was nationwide but again threw up some fascinating differences between Leave and Remain voters, who tend to value different leadership qualities. Remain voters placed most importance on integrity and softer attributes such as being a good listener and having empathy, while Leave voters favoured decisiveness, having conviction and being tough. As we have seen, our Red Wall voters were more likely to be Leave voters, and their patterns of preference followed this model. Michelle, chatting in the back of her butty shop in Accrington, explained that she wanted a leader who was 'for the working class', telling me that this meant being 'tough on the people who didn't want to work'. Kenneth, the retired butcher from Oswaldtwistle, felt that a good leader also needed to offer hope and be positive and patriotic. Graham Jones, the Labour MP who lost his Hyndburn seat, agreed that leadership is vital. His analysis of the Tories' success is simply that 'people were desperate to vote for a leader: it was all about leadership'. He suggested that now 'Labour needs someone of Blair's stature' to win again, adding, 'They need to recognise the problem but also have some clear vision of what's needed – and this cannot just be a 'retail offer'. He believes that means building an equal relationship with working-class voters, like those in Hyndburn, Stoke and Darlington. 'If they think you're a bit sniffy, you'll never get them back.'

In the BritainThinks study, we explored the views of many well-known leaders from history, sport and business and international figures as well as those from the UK. Consistent with previous surveys, we found that Winston Churchill is the highest scoring leader, evoking a strong sense of national pride as well as being considered effective. Other highly regarded individuals included Nelson Mandela, Steve Jobs, Margaret Thatcher and Alex Ferguson, as well as top-scoring Attenborough and Obama. Contemporary domestic politicians performed relatively poorly, clustering at the least effective end of the bar chart. Boris Johnson led this pack, followed by Nicola Sturgeon, Nigel Farage, Sadiq Khan, Jo Swinson, Theresa May and, right at the bottom of the pile, Jeremy Corbyn. Few inspired confidence. When we delved deeper and tested a wide range of attributes, including 'would represent Britain well on the international stage', 'would grow the economy', 'would take the right decisions in the interests of national security', and 'understands people like me', the response 'don't know' emerged as the winner by some distance. As voters grew more and more concerned about national division, expectations that these leaders could unite the country – or even their own party – were also lamentably low.

Jeremy Corbyn entered the 2019 election campaign in a very different place than that of 2017 when up against Theresa May, who, after initially framing the election campaign about Brexit, went on to make it all about herself. She proved to be a very poor campaigner, and this was reflected in rapidly declining voter ratings. When asked their views of her at the start of the 2017 campaign, voters chose words like 'calm', 'credible' and 'strong'. Joan from Birmingham paid her the ultimate compliment for any Tory leader: 'She's strong. She reminds me very much of Margaret Thatcher.' However, just a couple of weeks into the campaign and after a series of calamities, all that had changed. The words voters now chose included 'poor', 'struggling' and 'evasive'. By contrast, Corbyn looked good. One voter commented, 'Corbyn's words were in more plain, everyday English, whereas Theresa May appeared flustered at times and continued to speak as if she had swallowed her party's manifesto.' Corbyn's rating steadily improved from the start, where he had been written off as 'well-meaning but weak'. Now he was the calm one and had improved his performance so much that the focus group verdict was that he had run 'an excellent campaign'. In short, he exceeded very low expectations while Theresa May floundered.

But just two years later all that changed dramatically. Jeremy Corbyn found himself going into the election campaign with the worst personal ratings of any Leader of the Opposition since polling started measuring such things: a shocking net negative of -60 per cent. Focus groups in the intervening period had become increasingly bleak for the Labour leader. He was seen to preside over a disintegrating party. Many did not fully understand the term anti-Semitism, but they certainly knew that it was a bad thing and, crucially, that he had failed to resolve it, dividing his party further. This was, in many ways, though, the least of his problems. Corbyn was simply not seen as prime ministerial. Asked to sum him up in a word, the one most often chosen was 'scruffy'. Asked to describe what career he might have had if he had not been in politics, he was made an archaeologist or a geography teacher, two roles selected for their lack of sartorial elegance. Gareth Snell told me that people in Stoke often complained 'about Jeremy not shining his shoes'. They saw this as a personal slight:

> They expect you to be dressed appropriately for the office you hold. My grandad was a T&G [Transport and General Workers' Union] rep in the local chicken factory. He would come home of a Friday, shower and slick his hair then put on a suit and tie – his good suit. Stoke still has that mentality.

In short, people felt that Jeremy Corbyn was not fit to represent them. In fact, I'm told that considerable effort had gone into smartening up Corbyn's appearance, but once views are formed, they are hard to shake off – voters are not watching every move, just enough to decide what they think. From that point, confirmation bias kicks in: people simply tend to gather evidence to support their existing view and resist changing it.

As the 2019 election drew nearer and the problems surrounding Brexit became more acute – especially important to Red Wall voters – their judgement became harsher still. Most were Leave voters who resented that Labour did not support their view or even looked down on them for holding it. For Corbyn, this was also seen as a failure of leadership. They had wanted him to make a case, even if they disagreed with it. Asked which fictious character Corbyn was most like, 'Where's Wally' was the focus group answer. By failing to take a clear position one way or another, or even saying how he personally would vote in the second referendum that his own party was recommending, he had effectively absented himself from the debate, and they found this hard to forgive in a national leader.

When I asked the Red Wall voters how Labour had lost their vote, while Jeremy Corbyn was, of course, not the only reason, his role was clearly significant. He was almost always mentioned first, provoking a gale of often angry responses. Karen in Stoke explained that 'he made it almost impossible to vote Labour. I'd have done pretty much anything to stop him being Prime Minister.' Graham Jones, the losing MP in Hyndburn, told me that 'the Corbyn effect' was mentioned on the doorstep in four out of five cases. Jenny Chapman in Darlington felt the same: 'In

2017 he was just a bit harmless and daft but well-meaning, but by 2019 they were afraid of him. I got "he's a terrorist" on every other doorstep.' Certainly Corbyn was mentioned negatively by almost everyone at some point in my Red Wall interviews. For some it was simply: 'I just didn't like him.' Others struggled to imagine him as Prime Minister and were horrified at the thought of him representing the country abroad. There was also the sense of a relentless shift to the left that many disagreed with. He confirmed their belief that Labour was old-fashioned; he seemed old-fashioned himself and many of the policies he championed seemed like yesterday's solutions: 'Renationalising everything – it's just going backwards! Don't they remember how bad things used to be?' There were also significant concerns about Labour's economic policy – concerns that seemed borne out by the 'wishlist' manifesto. All this combined to make Corbyn seem like living proof of the fact that the Labour Party was no longer the party for people like them. Instead it was a party 'for the south' or for 'students and kids'. Most of all, for someone patriotic like Kenneth the retired butcher, Corbyn seemed to 'talk the country down, not up' and, worse still, he might have a tendency to 'stick up for people who are the enemies of Britain rather than our friends'. In 2017, the tabloids had tried hard to land an attack that criticised Corbyn for his foreign policy. 'Jezza's Jihadi Comrades' was *The Sun*'s eve-of-poll headline, while the *Mail* devoted thirteen pages describing Corbyn, Abbott and McDonnell as 'apologists for terror'. Focus groups at the time suggested this hadn't worked and that voters had given the Labour leadership the benefit of the doubt but, by 2019, it seemed the media's argument had gradually filtered through.

While voters were forming their views about Jeremy Corbyn's shortcomings, Theresa May was limping off stage and the Tories were choosing a new leader. Boris Johnson was already well known to many voters and, in the aftermath of Brexit, he looked to be a divisive figure. Again, the sharp divide split along Leave/Remain lines. Asked which animal he was most like, Leave voters chose a mighty lion or an eagle, while Remainers saw something much less attractive and much less trustworthy, like a snake or a fox. A similar divide transpired when asked which fictious character he most closely resembled. Leavers described a dynamic – even dashing – James Bond: a man of action who gets things done. Remainers were more circumspect, however. To them he was dangerously chaotic, Homer Simpson let loose in the control room and frantically asking, 'Which button was I meant to press?'

If Johnson's reputation had been variable during the election campaign, looking back afterwards, while he is still not everyone's cup of tea, a more consistent view has emerged. Paradoxically, some of his weaknesses now came across as strengths. His bumbling, disorganised demeanour lends him an authenticity that is rare in politicians. In my interviews, some thought it meant that he was actually very canny: 'buffoon' was the word most often used to describe him, but most concluded that the superficial image belied a shrewdness. Julie from Darlington saw it like this: 'Yes, he acts like a buffoon. He does daft things but he's smart!' Colin from Stoke thought he 'looks like a clown but he knows what he's doing', while Michelle from Accrington thought he 'likes people' and his willingness to 'play the fool' spoke to an admirable honesty. Most of all, his charisma and confidence – mentioned by so many people – translated into a positive, optimistic outlook for the whole country that some found to be contagious. 'Boris may be a plonker, but you feel like he's talking to you and he's positive, upbeat. He makes you feel up.' It was this feeling that gave some of my Red Wall voters a spring in their step: 'I think he cares about the country and believes he can make it better. I'll go with that.'

Expectations of Johnson were more muted in the wider country immediately post-election. 'I just think things are pretty much at rock bottom as they are. I keep thinking they can't get worse, but they probably can,' grumbled one voter in BritainThinks' research the following week. We had returned to hear from people who had been undecided in the campaign but who had eventually chosen Tory, and we found that many were willing Johnson to grow into the job, to become 'more grown-up and more suitable as a representative of Britain on the international stage'. The Red Wall voters, however, had dared to dream. Having taken the momentous decision to vote Tory, their expectations were now high. By March I was told that Johnson would bring the weaving sheds back into use in Accrington, reopen the mills, extend Darlington station, improve transport links across the whole of the north, create youth clubs and training opportunities, get us making things again. And growing things. And fishing things. It's a long wish-list and, when combined with their post-Brexit hopefulness, suggests that Johnson will need to be very clear indeed about what he can deliver, and then do so. In his favour so far is that the one promise of which everyone is aware ('get Brexit done') has, in their eyes, been achieved. Whether they voted Leave or Remain, back in January they felt grateful for that.

But politics doesn't stand still. So much of the analysis in this book ultimately falls into two camps: pre-Covid-19 and post-Covid-19. As things stand, it seems likely that whatever Johnson achieves in terms of post-Brexit delivery to the Red Wall, and however much he ups his game as a more grown-up, statesmanlike leader, in the end he will be judged for his handling of the UK's response to the pandemic. At the start of the crisis, the indications looked positive for Johnson. Immediately after he left hospital after succumbing to the disease himself, Johnson's positive leadership ratings improved to a high of 66 per cent according to YouGov. The electorate initially felt nothing but warmth towards him, the personification of the nation's struggle with the virus. But as he struggled to get back into the cut and thrust of day-to-day politics, those ratings began to slide in the wrong direction. Some weeks later it would appear that those numbers represented a high point from which the only way to go is down.

Leadership is a relative game in British politics, and it is clearly relatively easy to get ahead when you are up against the most unpopular Leader of the Opposition since polling began. However, on 4 April, Keir Starmer was elected Labour leader. Although it could hardly have been a more difficult time for him to make an impression with the public, he immediately improved on Corbyn's ratings (faint praise perhaps) and his own approval ratings initially kicked off at 39 per cent, a net positive score of +5 per cent, with much to play for, as 44 per cent of the electorate still had to make up their minds. The Stoke focus groups were the only ones conducted after Starmer's appointment. They had seen little of him and had yet to form a view. As care worker Jean observed, 'I feel for him in some ways because politics is on hold for now. He's got a long road ahead. Think how long the last four weeks has seemed. Four years is a lifetime away.'

13

WHY THE ECONOMY MATTERS

'They've got to be realistic. You can offer the earth but
how are you going to pay for it? We're not idiots!'

If being the least popular leader is barrier number one to
winning an election, not being trusted to run the economy
efficiently is probably barrier number two. While correlating
less perfectly with electoral success than leadership (Labour
only managed to narrow, rather than close, the gap between
themselves and the Conservatives ahead of the 1997 landslide),
being judged economically competent really, really matters. As
I set out in my 2010 review of Labour's years in government,
Talking to a Brick Wall, economic competency issues had
contributed significantly to Labour's long stint in opposition
in the 1980s and 1990s. It was crucial to change that negative
reputation with a carefully tested set of policies featuring, at its
heart, a pledge not to raise taxes – the voters' greatest fear about
Labour following the Tories' successful 1992 'double whammy

tax rise' attack. By 2001, Labour had taken a commanding lead in managing the economy, which it then held on to. Arguably, it was the economy that kept Labour in government in the otherwise difficult post-Iraq election of 2005. However, by 2010, Tory attacks on Labour's role in the financial crisis, fairly or unfairly, had stuck, reminding those with long memories of the pre-1997 era. This was hugely damaging to Labour's electoral prospects and was to become a legacy that would haunt Labour in the years to come.

Paula Surridge also identifies 2010 as a turning point. She believes that the economy mattered much less with some voters in post-2010 elections than it did in '97. In '97, she explains, the two main parties were seen as very different on the economically left–right axis, while it mattered much less where potential Labour voters sat on the liberal–authoritarian axis: back then they all voted Labour in the same proportion. By 2019, the historically Labour-voting working class saw those liberal–authoritarian values as a differentiator. However, this did not mean that the economy was not a factor in 2019. Surridge feels that there is a further warning in her work: it is not just culture and values that were a problem for Labour; voters who left the party were also further to the centre than Labour was on the economic left–right axis. 'I feel that's something that Labour haven't quite got to grips with,' she told me.

> In terms of the result of 2019. All the voters that they lost, whichever direction they went in, were more centrist – I don't like that word but they were more towards the centre

on left–right economic issues than those who stuck, so [Labour] are now losing votes because of their economic position as well.

This makes sense to me. My post-election analysis of public opinion after the 2015 election concluded that unwillingness to trust Labour to run the economy was one of the main reasons for defeat. Voters called out what they saw as Labour's dismal record. Even though seven years had passed, the banking crisis was still fresh in their minds and conflated with a long-held belief about Labour's tendency to overspend. Miliband's leadership had not managed to reassure. It was as if the banking crisis had pulled back a curtain on the Labour government's management of the economy, revealing – or reminding – them of a terrible truth. One man in Nuneaton summed up all the focus groups I'd listened to:

I think the banking crisis brought it all home, didn't it? I don't think in 2005 people knew how much we were borrowing; the numbers are so big they just sort of washed over your head. I think when the banking crisis happened and it started to hurt everybody, it started to come out how we just had no money and we were just borrowing and borrowing, and borrowing. I think they managed to get away with what they were doing for so long because things felt good.

By December 2019, the Tories enjoyed a 24 per cent lead on 'best policies for managing the economy' according to Ipsos MORI.

Reviewing Labour's catastrophic performance more than thirty years after I sat through my first ever focus group for Labour in 1986, hearing how profligate voters imagined a Labour government would be, it felt as if depressingly little had changed. Over that period the default voter view of Labour's economic performance was dominated by three beliefs, each one extremely unhelpful and with the potential to cause deep reputational damage. Firstly, many thought Labour's poor relationship with one of the key drivers of a successful economy, business, would severely handicap economic growth in a Labour administration. Secondly, there was a belief that Labour would spend taxpayers' hard-earned money irresponsibly, with at best damaging and at worst terrifying consequences. And lastly, many felt that Labour's spending priorities would mean a focus on the wrong people, encouraging the undeserving rather than the hard-working.

The Red Wall has a very particular perspective on all this. As well as sharing more generalised concerns about Labour's potential to wreck the economy, Red Wallers have significant concerns about the way money that *is* spent is targeted. Many feel that investment does not benefit them or the area in which they live. One of the men in an Accrington focus group summed up everyone's views: 'I've always voted Labour, but this time I sat down and thought hard about it. Can you tell me exactly what Tony Blair did for the north in three terms as Prime Minister?' BritainThinks' 2019 Mood of the Nation study found 69 per cent of people in Yorkshire, 65 per cent in the north-west and 64 per cent in the north-east agree that 'other areas in the UK get more funding and investment than my area', while only 30 per cent of Londoners believe that to be true. Shifting the balance of spending in favour of the north was a recurring theme in many people's future wish-lists. There was some awareness, though little understanding, of the Northern Powerhouse. There was a passionate belief that the economy had long been managed for the benefit of the south, especially London, and a passionate belief that this must change.

As we have seen, many of the Red Wall towns have a proud industrial heritage that has been devastated in the living memory of its residents. Reminders of the glory days are everywhere: the mills, the mines, the factories, the railway stations. Some of these buildings have been repurposed – as shopping malls, flats, arts centres or, more poignantly, museums – but many more lie boarded up and decaying, angry reminders of the area's decline. This had had a personal impact on almost everybody I spoke to. Several of the women, in the lowest-paid positions in retail or caring, were working two or three jobs to make ends meet. For the carers, almost half of the women in every focus group I ran, council cuts were impacting both their ability to actually work – given that many had family caring responsibilities – and their wages and terms of employment. Celia, a carer from Accrington, was so pressurised that she had to take two calls during the hour-and-a-half-long focus group, one to her elderly father-in-law, and one to an adult she was paid to care for. Many of the men I spoke to had endured extended periods of redundancy. A typical comment was: 'There used to be lots of jobs round here. You used to walk out of one job and into another but not any more.'

Red Wallers are not alone in feeling concerned about the economy. BritainThinks' Mood of the Nation study in the summer of 2019 showed that 56 per cent of the population felt pessimistic about the future of the economy, while just 32 per cent felt optimistic. People are aware of national statistics (GDP, unemployment data etc.) but don't understand them well and don't always trust them. Instead, they look around them for evidence of whether the economy is thriving or not. Symbols of failure include the decline of the high street – felt everywhere but particularly acutely in the Red Wall constituencies, who have lost their M&S and other 'quality' outlets in favour of pound shops, pawnbrokers and kebab joints. Some 78 per cent agree that 'more shops will close than open on my local high street in the next year or so'. They also notice poverty: people begging, foodbanks, homeless people, kids hanging around on street corners and boarded-up buildings. It was found that 68 per cent are pessimistic about poverty in their local area.

In May 2018, BritainThinks published a piece of research in collaboration with the *Financial Times*, exploring the public's views on business and on both main parties' economic reputations. The work confirmed the Tories as the party of business, especially big business. Despite the negative associations with 'fat cats' in pin-striped suits, business is seen as vital to the economy by most ordinary voters. One man in Southampton said, 'The country has to grow. If we don't grow, we'll get left behind. Business success has a knock-on effect all the way through the system.' The same evening, a female voter observed, 'The more business is making a profit, the more it is adding to the system. Businesses mean employment.' The study found that 58 per cent felt concerned that British business was struggling in the tough global trading environment. Meanwhile, 82 per cent said that they wanted the government to do more to support business and 58 per cent agreed that UK government should do more to regulate business. If it comes to a battle of trust between business and politicians, though, business wins hands down. Business is thought to be more 'in touch' with the general public than politicians (63 per cent vs 9 per cent), and more trusted (54 per cent vs 8 per cent).

The Tories have always been seen as the best party for big business – in the 2018 poll, 55 per cent vs Labour at 21 per cent – and, crucially, in the same poll, as the best party for the economy. Many voters in our focus groups credited the Conservatives with having rescued the economy from Labour, post the financial crisis. The Tory Party was seen as more ambitious, even ruthless in its aim. However, there was a sense in 2018 that the Tories under Theresa May were failing to build a successful strategy out of this natural advantage. This was partly about May's ineffectual approach to Brexit – known to be causing deep anxiety and uncertainty amongst business – and partly about the disastrous 2017 election campaign, where, in an attempt to marginalise Chancellor Philip Hammond, the economy was allowed to slip off the table. The BritainThinks poll found that just 39 per cent could name Hammond. Back in the days of the Labour government, Chancellor Gordon Brown was universally well known and as important a figure to the Labour Party's reputation as Prime Minister Tony Blair.

In the same 2018 poll, when voters thought about what Labour's approach to the economy might mean for them, the party's reputation took a further nosedive. It was seen as well-meaning but too eager to please – the image chosen in focus groups was a dog begging on its hind legs. In its eagerness, Labour was also seen as naïve, likely to over-promise and then not deliver. This becomes more acute when the economy is linked to business, magnifying the long-standing concerns of many voters. One man told us: 'Labour are frightening. If they came to power they would just spend with no thought about the consequences.' This took me back to the period I spent advising Gordon Brown as he developed and executed his 'Prudence' strategy of fiscal restraint. It had been vital in getting Labour into power in the first place and continued to be vital as the party undertook the work of government. Proving Labour's competency had been difficult, and we had worked hard to find a convincing message. Brown, Labour's popular and reassuring messenger, had been mission critical too. By 2018, much of this thinking had been forgotten.

At first sight, many of Labour's 2017 manifesto policies had looked attractive. We tested them blind in polling and focus groups. There, 61 per cent favoured increasing the minimum wage to £10: 'Sounds like a good idea,' observed one voter, 'if you look at companies in the High Street. Poundland, for example – all their staff are on the minimum wage.' Another 58 per cent approved of more help for small businesses (e.g. lower corporation tax and reform to punishing business rates). We found that 55 per cent favoured strengthening workers' rights (such as banning zero-hour contracts and increasing trade union powers) and 55 per cent supported tax rises on the top 5 per cent of earners (defined as more than £70,000 per year). There was much less marked support for policy areas that voters judged would actively harm business, however. Fewer than four out of ten supported working towards a 20:1 pay ratio between the highest- and lowest-paid workers and fining businesses that exceed this, and only a quarter supported raising corporation tax up to 26 per cent. One voter protested strongly: 'I think we shouldn't concentrate on squeezing tax out of British companies...'

Renationalisation was also a grey area. While at face value there was modest support – 46 per cent said they'd like to see 'rail, water and the Post Office back in government ownership' – there were powerful reservations about this being a very costly policy area and therefore not a priority. 'It sounds like a good idea, but it would be so expensive. Where is the money coming from?' asked one. We also found that some industries like rail are more top of mind as candidates for nationalisation because of their perceived failings, while those like water are less pressing.

In spite of all this, while many of these policies fared well enough when tested blind and individually, support plummeted when the policy area was associated with Labour. It fell even further when the policies were presented collectively as a package, rather than individually. Suddenly all Labour's negative economic baggage came to the fore and voters, previously enthusiastic, began to visibly cool, suddenly doubting whether the policies made sense. 'They sound good on paper, but Labour needs to get out their calculator.'

Of course, the economic policies on offer from Labour in 2017 were very much less ambitious than those the party put forward in 2019. At first sight, therefore, it was rather to Labour's advantage that Ashcroft's 2019 election tracker showed how little people picked up from the campaign. The week that the manifestos were launched, just 10 per cent said they had noticed them at all, while 39 per cent said they'd seen 'nothing' and 10 per cent said they'd noticed only politicians' 'lies'. However, as the campaign unfolded, BritainThinks' analysis suggested that, while individual policies lacked cut through, there was a general sense that Labour had an unrealistic proliferation of policies, and all this confirmed their existing views that Labour couldn't be trusted and would tend to serve up unrealistic and unfunded policies. When we asked voters to choose a song to sum up Labour's campaign, they went for 'Highway to the Danger Zone', saying, 'They're offering us unicorns' with unaffordable, 'fanciful spending policies'. Labour were revealing their tendency to be impractical, even naïve. Most voters were unaware of any evidence supporting or opposing individual policies, instead responding to them instinctively and tending to judge them negatively. The Labour brand even tainted those that might have had superficial appeal, such as a four-day week: 'If we're operating on four days of work and everyone else is doing five, we're not going to be in a strong position globally,' one focus group member observed.

These sentiments were echoed in Hyndburn, Darlington and

Stoke-on-Trent. Jenny Chapman, Darlington's outgoing MP, believes that, while the party's empathy problems are real and need to be addressed, the far bigger problem is competency. 'It's like the party was careering out of control. People felt afraid. We were irrational. Things like offering free broadband, which people were confused about and no one said they wanted, or the uncosted WASPI women pensions pledge, just served to reinforce this.' Graham Jones, former MP in Hyndburn, agreed. Although he felt that the policy offer mattered less than the leadership, he was scornful of the 'vacuous manifesto' and felt that the party had displayed its lack of understanding of an electorate like his with its vast sweep of policies – its 'retail offer'. Similarly, Gareth Snell, the former MP in Stoke-on-Trent, felt that Labour's fiscal approach was at odds with the way his constituents ran their own family budgets – and they knew someone was going to pay for it: 'The more money we said we'd spend, the more they thought their taxes would go up.' At a local level, this concern was amplified by people's sense that the local council also 'chucked money around', as Sean, an electrician from Stoke, described it.

Meanwhile, though many commentators were critical of the Conservatives' 'policy lite' manifesto, it seemed that they, determined not to repeat the mistakes of their unpopular 2017 manifesto, had judged this right. In policy terms, voters generally judge that less is more. I was reminded of the extensive time I spent testing the handful of policies that featured on Labour's pledge card in 1997, each symbolic of a wider policy intent but disciplined in its scope. By two weeks into the campaign, when I asked voters 'what would Labour do if they won power', most were able to trot out all five pledges, having learned them by heart. Asking the same question in 2019, I was met by silence, then a vague 'spend more money'. Meanwhile, according to Ashcroft's tracker, Boris Johnson's modest policy pledge of 50,000 more nurses did seem to have cut through by the final fortnight, kept in the news by a somewhat technical row about whether this number was about new nurses or simply retaining the ones we already have. But, of course, the policy that people noticed most was the Conservatives' one really significant promise – arguably the biggest spending pledge of all – 'Get Brexit done!'

This, when combined with the ongoing assumption that Labour is not on your side if you are an ordinary voter who works hard and wants to get on, becomes a toxic mix. These are long-held, hard-to-shift views. Back in 1992, I worked on the Southern Discomfort project for the Fabian Society with distinguished Labour MP Giles Radice as we set out to understand why voters in southern seats had rejected Labour. It was the party that would make them worse off, we were told. Labour was 'out to clobber you'. It was also the party that, in 2010, dismissed Mrs Duffy and her concerns about workers from Europe undercutting workers' wages in her area as 'that bigoted woman'. And it was the party that, in 2015, seemed only on the side of the most needy – at the massive expense of the people whom Theresa May branded the 'jams': the just about managing. Many of the people I listened to in the Red Wall were barely managing at all and felt an extraordinary

resentment when they assumed that funds were being diverted away from them, often to the less deserving. Many would
have been recipients of benefits, but this if anything made them
more eager to distinguish their position from that of those they
would dismiss as work-shy. Only the much better-off can enjoy
the luxury of generosity. Julie, the part-time cleaner from Darlington, felt sure that the Labour Party would spend too much
time and money – her money – on people who simply didn't
want to work.

This still begs the question of why the Conservatives – previously seen by voters like Michelle from Accrington as 'snobby,
just for the posh' – would be so trusted to run the economy
well and in the interests of these lifelong Labour voters. I think
the answer lies in the Conservatives successfully outscoring
Labour on the three grievances that have haunted it over the
past four decades: having a positive relationship with business;
thus having the credibility to build a strong economy, spending
carefully; and not being overly focused on the 'undeserving'
poor at the expense of ordinary working people. Even so, as
we approached the election in 2019, there were signs that the
public was even more weary of austerity than it had been in
2017. Ipsos MORI found that 56 per cent believed 'the government should increase spending on public services even if that
means higher taxes or borrowing'. Only 10 per cent wanted the
government to reduce spending to allow for tax cuts or less
borrowing.

Labour believed that their moment had come. They saw
the chance to build on the apparent success of 2017 by ending

austerity while the Conservatives would be punished for creating it. However, during the election campaign, Boris Johnson joined Jeremy Corbyn in declaring that 'austerity is over'. In fact, he told *The Spectator* that he had always felt the flagship economic policy of the Cameron government was 'not the right way forward for the UK', saying, 'I always thought, why use the language of [the Labour Chancellor responsible for post-war rationing] Stafford Cripps?' With both parties advocating ending savage public spending cuts, the decision facing voters was who would be most trusted to deliver the economy they wanted to see. It seemed that the unravelling of Labour's hard-won economic advantage, which had started with the financial crisis in 2010, was now complete. The Conservatives remained doggedly ahead.

PART THREE

WHAT DO RED WALLERS WANT?

14

HOPES FOR THE FUTURE

'I've got my spark back again. I feel really positive about the future now. I think my grandson will have something to look forward to now...'

As is often the case with politics, there are two seemingly inconsistent things happening simultaneously when we ask voters what future change they hope to see. It's what psychologists call cognitive dissonance: where people can hold multiple contradictory views at the same time. Voters in focus groups can quickly generate a wish-list as long as your arm. Yet, at the same time, their expectations are so pitifully low, you could be forgiven for thinking it almost impossible not to exceed them. The wish-list derives from most voters' long-held dissatisfaction with the future direction of the country, while low expectations are the product of their belief that any politician's endeavours will likely end in failure. What people want loosely falls into three buckets: of course, they have hopes and dreams for themselves and their family; they also want to see change in their local area; and they have ambition for the country as a whole. According to BritainThinks' Mood of the Nation work, the start point for most people as they approached the 2019 election was the deepest possible pessimism about the country. Yet many were more positive about prospects for their own local area (although this positivity was sometimes hard to find in Red Wall areas like Hyndburn). All were significantly cheerier when thinking about their own lives. Overlaid on that is many Leave voters' giddy optimism about what the post-Brexit landscape could bring.

The latter overrides party vote. Kenneth, the affable retired butcher from Oswaldtwistle, told me that his new-found 'spark' had little to do with voting Conservative for the first time: 'I've never been very political. I didn't vote at all until I was well into my thirties. Couldn't see the point.' But now, he reckons, things are looking good – really good – for the first time in ages: 'Now we can make and set our own rules. We used to have the best of everything – engineering, agriculture, fisheries. And I think we can be the best again, and that will bring employment back.' Warming to his theme, he explained that 'now we're fully in control, manufacturing will come back. The weaving sheds round here – they're all closed down. Industry went away. Money went abroad. All that's going to change.' I asked, 'Was it Europe's fault that the weaving sheds closed down?' For the first time in our conversation Kenneth looked a little less certain. 'I don't know. I honestly don't know. I don't know the ins and outs of it, but what I do know is that it seems like it's going to get better.' 'What exactly will get better?' I pressed. 'Seas!' Kenneth, a keen angler, found his way onto surer ground here. 'The fishermen in Cornwall had to stick to ridiculous quotas. It's been a huge issue. They had to throw away their surplus. It's a terrible waste of fish.' I asked, 'Will it affect butchery?' Again, Kenneth's first answer was somewhat hesitant. He wasn't sure. His former boss tended to buy New Zealand lamb anyway. 'Why not English lamb?' I asked. 'Too many EU regulations, I think,' he replied, his certainty returning. 'So that will change for sure?'

Julie from Darlington was feeling pretty positive too: 'If we're more independent we'll have more jobs.' Her take was less about investing in manufacturing and more about 'stopping immigrants from coming here' as a route to 'being self-sufficient – we should means test possible immigrants and only allow in those who can fund themselves and who have the skills that we definitely need'. The other reason to be cheerful was 'getting back the payments to the EU'. This, she thought, could fund the changes she'd like to see and, for the first time, the UK will be able to invest in the right areas without being dictated to by Europe. Ronnie, a bus driver from Stoke-on-Trent, agreed: 'Two things, really – we'll be able to get a grip on immigration, and we'll get our money back.' Even Bob, the Darlington-based painter and decorator who had actually voted Remain, now felt pretty hopeful about what might come next: 'We've had three years of dilly-dallying, now we can move forward and focus on the things that matter. And I'm confident that will mean more investment in areas like this and not before time.'

This investment imperative highlights one of the most consistent Red Waller aspirations: to end what they often describe in shorthand as the north–south divide – a phenomenon they believe has favoured the south for so long and must now be resolved. I asked my focus groups to work in pairs drafting up a vision for a successful future and this point was made by almost every couple: 'We need to shift power north,' asserted Ian and Gary from Accrington, while Gordon demanded, 'Invest in infrastructure and manufacturing all round the country, not just down south.' This is, most instinctively feel, a zero-sum game. Most reckon it's impossible for everybody in the country to do better. Funds must be diverted away from the south so that the Midlands and the north can have their fair share of the good fortune that has eluded them for too long. BritainThinks' Mood of the Nation survey from summer 2019 clearly identified the problem that Red Wallers now feel is on the way to being fixed. Nationally, half were convinced that 'other areas in the UK receive more funding and investment than my own'. This rises to two-thirds in Red Wall areas but is less than one-third in London. The resentment is palpable.

But what do voters actually need to see to believe the change they want is happening and funds really are coming their way? During the early New Labour years, the challenge of providing proof points was something that greatly preoccupied those working on the project. The whole endeavour had started as the 1997 election approached, with the quest to find 'symbolic policies' – tangible policy outcomes that were effective in themselves but that were also a shorthand for the party's broader philosophy or beliefs. Mrs Thatcher's 'right to buy' had been the perfect example of this (however imperfect it turned out to be in its long-term impact on the housing market). Giving people in council housing the right to buy their property made many voters' dreams come true but was also clear evidence of Mrs Thatcher's small-state ideology at work. It combined fulfilling individual aspiration with the government's wider vision, while also addressing what was then the Tory Party's greatest electoral handicap: being 'out of touch' with working-class voters. Boris Johnson's approach to Brexit may well have achieved the same. Despite subsequent failures of the housing market that some would say stem from Thatcher's decision, and the resulting reduction in available social housing, and despite little affection for Mrs Thatcher herself in many parts of the Red Wall, the right to buy is still frequently and positively namechecked in focus groups there almost forty years later.

Despite a lengthy policy review process, Labour never found its one killer policy in 1997. Instead, it settled for the five policies that made up the pledge card. Each of the five related to a crucial policy area and we tested and retested them to find the most compelling promise for each. As well as distributing a physical card, all campaigning (leaflets, ads, broadcasts etc.) focused on these five pledges. By half-way through the 1997 campaign, I found that people in focus groups could recite the content of the pledge card back to me. Sure, the policies themselves were popular, but closer examination told us people's votes were less about guarantees of smaller class sizes, shorter hospital waiting lists, or fast-tracking of young offenders, and more about the promise of a different way of doing politics. The pledge card symbolised just that. It offered specifics that addressed voters' concerns about the NHS and schools, while at the same time neatly addressing their concerns about Labour – laying to rest their worry that Labour would offer the earth and not be held accountable. The pledge card itself became the symbolic policy, reducing the manifesto down to five crisp pledges. It would, we assumed, be easy to judge whether or not these had been delivered.

However, several years down the track and after raising taxes and injecting funds to revive the ailing public services, we began to see a strange and unexpected phenomenon. The government had heeded advice about the need for 'quick wins' and there had been intense focus on the services that were at the top of voters' wish-lists: cleaner hospitals, shorter A&E waiting times, faster appointments for critical treatments like cancer surgery. People were seeing the change with their own eyes, feeling the impact on their own lives, and yet, frustratingly, they were not extrapolating this experience out to draw a wider conclusion about improvements in the services they used. Instead, drawing as they did on news reports and anecdotal evidence, they presumed that their own good fortune was not part of a wider trend but a fortunate, isolated fluke. Voters would explain it away: 'I took my daughter to A&E and we were seen pretty quickly, but we were lucky.' Or: 'My son's school is really good – we're very lucky.' We had not predicted what we came to describe as 'I've been Lucky Syndrome'. It was reflected in all our polling too, which highlighted a gap between the perception of general public services and 'my' public services, the latter scoring more highly but failing to impact on the growing dissatisfaction with the government, as people dismissed their personal good fortune.

There will be many challenges in achieving credible and visible investment in Red Wall seats. Though there are common themes that affect them all (poor connectivity, shortage of good jobs, decaying high streets, lack of parks, lack of youth facilities), they also all have distinctive and strongly felt needs. Nonetheless it seems reasonable to suppose that new infrastructure projects would be a good start. That said, for all the billions that HS2 will soak up, it may very well not hit the spot. I heard scepticism from some Red Wallers concerned that, once again, this policy might deliver more for London than their local area. Speeding up local rail links (for example, addressing the one-hour, twenty-minute journey to cover the twenty miles to Manchester from Accrington) might be more effective. Peter Gibson, new MP for Darlington, acknowledged that the rail links from his constituency to London are already excellent. He was much more worried about local connections, pointing out that Darlington station has already reached full capacity. He had been campaigning for investment to build two new platforms and, as noted earlier, this was to prove a 'quick win'. His lobbying resulted in a cash promise in Rishi Sunak's first Budget in March 2020, although Gibson would have been disappointed at how little this had been noticed in Darlington focus groups and interviews less than a week later. Bob shrugged when I asked him if he had noticed the Budget. However, he had noticed Rishi Sunak's arrival on the scene. Perhaps anticipating Sunak's swift rise in popularity as the government's response to Covid-19 got underway, Bob was unequivocal: 'I like him. I warm to him. A local lad.' I pointed out that Sunak comes from Southampton and that his constituency is Richmond, Yorkshire. 'That's local enough for me,' Bob insisted.

As we have seen, many Red Wallers share concern about the long-term decline of their place. This was a consistent theme, too, in the citizens' jury that BritainThinks ran for Labour Together in March 2020. Voters from Red Wall constituencies outside Manchester and Leeds were often despairing about the decay of the public realm. 'It's a dump,' said Dave bluntly, talking about his hometown, Bolton. 'The first thing you see when you arrive here is boarded-up buildings and broken windows.' There is also a decline in the availability of what the think tank Onward describes as 'local assets': facilities for young people were an issue everywhere. The numbers of libraries are dwindling, too, as local activist Yvonne Richardson's battle to save the beautiful library in Darlington illustrated. But, assuming that funding priorities need to be established, arriving at the best possible set of priorities may be tricky. Getting it wrong can be higher risk than not bothering at all. In Accrington, everyone bemoans the decline of the shopping centre. But this is more about high-quality retailers like M&S opting out than it is about the building or infrastructure. Hyndburn Council's attempts to improve the entrance (as we've seen, described as 'bright yellow cornflakes set into black tar – it's a joke') got a massive thumbs down from the focus groups. In this instance, the people I spoke to suggested that they should have been consulted before the council spent their money – and maybe, at a local level, this is the way forward, connecting people more closely with the decisions that are taken on their behalf.

In the Labour Together citizens' jury, we began by asking participants what worried them in their personal lives, in their local area and for the country. We gave them a pre-task, asking them to keep a diary noting what 'kept them awake at night'. It was interesting to see how very different the worries of jurors from Red Wall areas were compared with jurors from the more urban locations of Manchester and London. While the latter tended to look outwards and generally had a more global take on the challenges ahead, the Red Wallers' concerns were more personal. Financial difficulties were often top of mind when thinking about their own circumstances. BritainThinks' Mood of the Nation survey found that a quarter of the population and a third of working-class voters were concerned that they wouldn't be able to pay for essentials in the coming year, and 45 per cent overall, rising to 55 per cent of the working class, were pessimistic about their future ability to pay for luxuries. Angie, a carer from Bolton and a juror in the Labour Together session, told me that she worked three jobs over six long days each week just to make ends meet. And even then, she often couldn't quite manage to balance the books. Her day off wasn't much of a break either, as she had to care for her 93-year-old grandma. No wonder that 'come the night-time, I'm tired and cranky'. She went on to say she felt that 'mental health' was a growing problem, caused by the stress of financial insecurity.

Work also feels more insecure now, and one in five say that this affects them directly. The Red Wall women I spoke to were particularly hard hit. Many, like Angie, were working multiple jobs, often a mix of caring roles and shop or call centre work (the latter usually on zero-hour contracts). All of the men bemoaned the loss of manufacturing work locally. Many of the men I listened to were self-employed, working as mechanics or in construction as decorators, electricians or plumbers. Most felt their livelihoods were tough – they had to put in long hours when the work was there – and precarious: the work often wasn't there. Others were worried about automation and AI: 'We're being replaced by robots,' said Dave, also from Bolton, while Renee expressed relief at being a midwife. 'A computer can't deliver a baby,' she said, 'but I can, so I reckon I'll always have a job.' Several had been forced to retrain – as we heard, Kenneth had been a butcher but at the end of his working life, after redundancy, had to learn to make furniture for the Senator Group, now Accrington's biggest employer. Bob became a painter and decorator after years of factory work and, before that, was in the army.

Yet, despite these difficulties in their personal circumstances, most of the people I met in the Red Wall were pretty positive when it came to their own lives. Kenneth felt fortunate to get another job and have the chance to learn something new in his late fifties. Bob had managed to build up a solid network of customers and was really enjoying volunteering with the scouts. Pride and pleasure are taken in the things that do go right; difficulties are dismissed with wry humour. Debra in

Accrington was typical: 'I collect my granddaughter from school most days. It can be a race to get there when I finish my job. It's hard work, too, but I love it. She's the light of my life!' Julie in Darlington had been made redundant from her full-time admin job a few months before and now worked part-time in 'a little cleaning job'. She described a hectic week of work, baby-sitting and dog-sitting for her children living nearby. 'I ask myself how ever did I find the time for full-time work,' she joked.

BritainThinks' final wave in the Brexit Diaries series, timed for after the 31 January deadline passed, found that 63 per cent felt Boris Johnson's deal meant a 'new era' for Britain – a triumphant 91 per cent of 'Die Hard' Leavers felt even more upbeat. People who had felt ignored, looked down on, judged and patronised finally felt listened to – their worldview at last in the ascendance, with the country led by someone who 'got them' and made clear promises that reflected that. Certainly, the optimism that I heard in Hyndburn, Darlington and Stoke-on-Trent bears this out, and so far that optimism feels vindicated because, in their eyes, after 31 January, Johnson has against the odds delivered on the one 'symbolic' pledge that he made: get Brexit done. The Red Wallers I spoke to were now eager to see what that might deliver for them. Looking forward, their ambition is high, even if the ask is often, for now, quite vague, vague in a way that may well be helpful to the Conservatives. Nonetheless, as Labour's experience shows, while benefit of the doubt may be awarded at first, when they come to pass judgement voters are likely to look for tangible proof, evidenced through their own experience, as well as through a sense of how their town and how the country as a whole is faring. Chris Powell, a wise old ad man who worked on Labour's 1997 campaign, once observed that, in the end, despite ad agencies' best efforts, there are only two election campaign slogans: 'Steady as we go' or 'Time for a change'. The Tories must hope to have made enough progress that voters buy into the first of these.

15

CAN LABOUR WIN THEM BACK?

'I do think their values are our values. I think we all think that.
But we're not talking about a little tweak here. They're going
to have to completely reinvent themselves.'

As I started writing, one of the big questions was, of course, whether these Red Wall seats could ever be winnable again for Labour, and, if so, what would it take? Listening to voters in Hyndburn, Darlington and Stoke-on-Trent, the overwhelming sense I had was that, while of course it would be possible for Labour to win again, winning may well be harder than even the most pessimistic Labour activists and politicians are expecting. Voting Labour had been a habit for many: a habit that, once broken, could be tricky to revive. Even with a new leader who is not the deeply unpopular Jeremy Corbyn, it is a tough ask. None of the Red Wallers I listened to were expecting to return any time soon. As we have seen, many felt taken for granted, even looked down on. James Kanagasooriam, who first coined the term 'Red Wall', observed dryly: 'Labour just lacks intellectual humility … they see voting Labour as a moral duty and that has led to a strategic blindness. Labour think they have a moral right to 50 per cent of the vote.' My former business partner, Philip Gould, in his brilliant account of Labour's road to victory in 1997, *The Unfinished Revolution*, summed up his exasperation at this attitude with a tongue-in-cheek remark: 'The electorate has voted against us four times. What's wrong with them?'

Lord Ashcroft's post-election polling highlights the gaping disconnect between party and potential voter. He found that 70 per cent of Labour members felt sure that people like these Red Wallers would return to Labour at the next election. Some 22 per cent thought this because they believed 2019 was only about Brexit. At 49 per cent, almost half presumed voters would come to fiercely dislike Tory government policies. Meanwhile, 76 per cent of those new Tory voters were clear that 'Labour will need to change very significantly' before they can consider voting that way again. Worse still from Labour's perspective, Ashcroft found that only 27 per cent of Labour-to-Tory voters like our Red Wallers could 'see themselves voting Labour in the future'. BritainThinks conducted follow-up interviews with similar people immediately after the 2019 election and heard the same story. While those votes were given to the Tories with wildly varying degrees of enthusiasm, it seems that, on the whole, they were *given*, not *lent*. BritainThinks' verdict in December was that those we spoke to were not expecting to return to Labour any time soon. Instead, they were waiting for Labour to 'completely reinvent themselves'. This, they imagined, might be a lengthy process. They were not holding their breath.

As if this was not enough, there was another significant challenge: even if it were possible to appease the disaffected Red Wall voter, was it possible to do this while also keeping faith with the voters – typically younger, educated, urban Remainers – who had stuck with Labour at its lowest ebb in 2019? Generals always fight the last war, as the saying goes. How big is the risk of losing 2019 Labour voters in a bid to win back Red Wallers? In March 2020, a few weeks ahead of the election of the new Labour leader, BritainThinks and Labour Together's citizens' jury put this to the test. We brought together representatives of these two very different Labour 'tribes': Red Wallers, recruited as town dwellers from constituencies that had voted Leave and abandoned Labour in 2019; and city-based Labour voters who had voted Remain and stuck with the party in the election, the 'Urban Remainers'. Our aim was to encourage both groups to share their views frankly, explore and debate differences and, ultimately, to try to identify common ground. It would form part of a package to be prepared for the new leader, once appointed, to help navigate the months ahead.

Citizens' juries are a methodology from the stable of research and engagement known as 'deliberative' research. The key features that differentiate them from mainstream research methods are that they provide participants with the information and time they need to make an informed contribution to a debate. As James Fishkin, pioneer of deliberative polling in the US, put it: 'An ordinary opinion poll can only tell you what people think, given how little they know.' Deliberative methods set out to show how citizens respond once made aware of potential trade-offs and given the time and guidance to support them through the decision-making process. This may involve providing information or exposure to other viewpoints as well as enabling debate.

We first met our eighteen jurors one Tuesday evening in March, amidst the faded glory of Manchester's Mechanics Institute, a traditional Victorian red-brick building in the heart of the city centre. It was the birthplace of the Trades Union Congress back in 1868 and we arrived through a grand hall displaying beautiful hand-made banners and sepia photographs depicting the workers' struggle through the years. We began by dividing our jurors into two discrete groups housed in two adjoining rooms, so they could initially develop their thinking surrounded by like-minded people before being thrown into the challenge of accommodating the needs of those whose worldview might be very different from their own. I joined the Red Wall group: people who had travelled in from nearby constituencies like Bolton or from places a little further afield, like Wakefield and Penistone and Stocksbridge. They included Angie, a foster carer and shopworker, Lila, a debt counsellor, Renee, a midwife, and Johnnie, who worked in sales.

Throughout that first evening we listened as they told us about their lives, describing a typical week with its highs and lows, frustrations and fun. We then asked them to play a game, pretending that they were setting up a new political party: one that was designed solely to meet the needs of people like them. They were to consider who the new party should represent; what its vision, values and policy priorities should be – and who might make the best leader. The results were fascinating. Our Red Wall jurors were emphatic that this party should be the party of the working class, basically people like them. The new, ideal party they designed that evening in Manchester drew on what they described as 'traditional Labour' values: equality and fairness, but also, importantly, honesty and transparency: 'Don't just say what you think people want to hear – you need to explain it, say this is why and make your case, make a decent argument,' argued Dave from Bolton. There was something else going on too: 'The party must be realistic,' Lila made her point forcefully, adding, 'Where Labour went wrong last time was promising lots of things that we knew they couldn't do. It has to be affordable and it has to be realistic.' Others agreed with this: 'Free Wi-Fi for everyone!' someone remembered, and the whole room laughed at the sheer folly of it all. The final element in the mix was yet another reference back to MPs' lack of understanding of how people like them live their lives. 'Our party would stick our MPs on a workers' wage,' Angie told me. 'An average of what ordinary people are on – and with realistic expenses as well. One of my jobs is fostering children, and when you do that every penny has to be accounted for.'

Team Red Wall's suggested policy offer, expressed as the first three laws their ideal party would pass in government, was next on the agenda. Their top priority happily turned out to be exactly the same as that simultaneously developed by the Urban

Remainers in the room next door: more cash for front-line services, particularly the NHS and the police. 'We could probably use the £350 million per week they talked about on the bus,' mused one Red Waller. After much discussion and a vote, the group arrived at a joint second place: social housing and immigration. The first of these would again prove to be a point of unity with the other group, as the Urban Remainers had also identified housing shortages and poor, over-priced private rentals as a major problem. The second, controlling immigration, declared a 'must-have' by Red Wallers, was to turn out, initially at least, to be a major obstacle to agreement when the two groups worked together. In third place, a review of tax and benefits was also common ground with both groups of jurors, but each identified slightly different problems to solve here. The Red Wallers were mostly preoccupied with dealing with scroungers: 'There's so many people on the make who know how to game the system,' was a typical comment. Meanwhile the Urban Remainers next door were more concerned with sorting out big corporate tax-dodgers. The Red Wallers added a further point – again placing them at odds with the Urban Remainers; they wanted to halt overseas aid. Angie explained, 'Charity begins at home – we have kids here that don't have enough to eat – why on earth are we sending money abroad? Madness!'

Perhaps the most telling element of the ideal party created by the Red Wallers was its choice of leader. Three candidates emerged that all claimed to be happy with. The first, Alan Sugar, 'because he's a billionaire who knows about business and running things. He'd bring real expertise to the country,' explained Renee from Bolton, while Angie added, 'You need someone with a business sense. You need to be able to negotiate. That's why Trump works, because he gets things done.' The second choice was everyone's favourite expert: finance hotshot Martin Lewis, chosen less for his expertise and more for his reputation as 'the people's finance advisor', speaking out on behalf of ordinary men and women in the face of big business. 'He's one of my heroes,' said David from Wakefield. Finally, there was a choice unanimously supported by the Red Wall team that would later prove controversial with the Urban Remainers: 'Tim Wetherspoon' as the group referred to him, meaning Tim Martin, the founder of Wetherspoon's pubs and a well-known Brexiteer. Dave eulogised, 'I love his pubs! He's been an advocate of Brexit too – very British. He pays his taxes, says it like it is – and his breakfasts are excellent!' On hearing this the next day, Simon, a London-based accountant from the other team, confided in me: 'I literally can't believe that I'm spending a whole day in the same room as a group of people who'd like that awful Wetherspoon's bloke to be Prime Minister.'

We were determined to find out what Labour reinventing itself might look like for the Red Wallers, but also to discover if it would be feasible to manage this reinvention while retaining the votes of the Urban Remainers (who had, incidentally, chosen as their 'ideal leader' a very different cast of characters: Michelle Obama, Hugh Grant, or 'a young David Attenborough'). We began with each group sharing their 'manifestos'.

At first sight, the two had much common ground in terms of outlook and values: both felt concerned that there are many people in the country struggling to get by without enough support – although this was a more abstract concern for many Urban Remainers than it was for Red Wallers, for whom financial hardship is often in their personal experience. All agreed that everyone should have the opportunity to get on and achieve success, and all agreed that, however they had voted, Brexit is now a reality and we need to 'get on with it'. There was also consensus that the NHS is our most highly valued institution and needs to be better resourced, along with other public spending priorities including social housing and the police (the latter being a higher priority for Red Wallers).

The choice of leader most vividly illustrated the differences between the two Labour tribes, but their carefully crafted campaign slogans, designed to 'sell' their ideal party, also dramatically highlighted their differences. Urban Remainers raised eyebrows at, though politely did not openly challenge, 'Make Britain Great Again'. They drafted 'Fairness for All' or 'Tomorrow's Future Today' instead. Red Wallers are, as we have seen, patriotic, and community-focused, often looking back with nostalgia to a 'golden past'. Fairness was interpreted from a personal perspective, reviewed in terms of what it might deliver for them and their families. The future was something they often felt anxious about. In contrast, Urban Remainers looked forward to the future with anticipation and tended to see Britain as intimately interconnected with the whole world. For them, fairness meant redistribution of wealth, certainly away from the wealthiest and probably away from them personally too – a luxury few Red Wallers felt they could afford.

The next step in the jury process was to mix up the two groups and encourage them to work together building a coalition between their two ideal parties. They took on the challenge with great gusto. Starting with the 'vision', reaching agreement about a set of words was deceptively easy. They quickly amalgamated the values both groups had espoused into 'Equality and Prosperity for a Fairer and Stronger Britain'. Also easy was setting out a demand for greater investment in the NHS, housing, education and police. There was even agreement on where the funds would come from: taxing big companies more (as one Urban Remainer observed, 'It's ridiculous that Amazon pay so little tax! I probably pay more tax than they do!') and also closing tax loopholes. Red Wallers were eager to see more money clawed back from 'scroungers' but could agree broadly to the Urban Remainers, 'ask' to increase benefits in line with the cost of living. Likewise, Urban Remainers were accepting of Red Wallers' desire that prosperity must be spread more widely across the country, through north and south, towns as well as cities.

As is often the case, the devil was in the detail. Initially, our groups, forced to work with people whose views did not coincide with their own, simply avoided confrontation. The Red Wallers' plans for ending overseas aid was quietly binned. Several of them muttered their disagreement, but in the face of impassioned pleas by the Urban Remainers, Red Wallers opted to choose a different battleground: immigration. They had, after all, made it the centrepiece of their manifesto and initially regarded it as 'non-negotiable', while the Urban Remainers had made a point of declaring that immigration is a 'positive contribution' to the country. Both groups now felt deeply uncomfortable. We were observing at first hand what American sociologist Arlie Hochschild calls the 'empathy wall': a wall that prevents us from understanding the point of view of another person, especially when we feel hostile towards these views. It struck me, though, observing participants feeling their way around this topic, that a more typical response when confronted with the other side may not be anger but avoidance. Both groups were afraid of being judged: Urban Remainers were worried about seeming out of touch with Red Wallers' concerns, while Red Wallers were silenced by the fear that they would be seen as racist (ironic from a group that had been complaining to each other about 'political correctness' stifling debate the evening before).

Observing these discussions as the day unfolded, it became clear that simply allowing the groups to park immigration, as they had opted to park ending overseas aid, risked ending up with a proposition with which neither could ever be satisfied. We decided to put this to the test by inviting all participants to vote individually for their policy priorities and, despite the fact that it had fallen off the prepared joint list, we added 'restricting immigration' back into the discussion. The results were fascinating. Immigration emerged as the second most voted for priority after investment in the NHS. The numbers revealed that some Urban Remainers must have voted for it.

Throughout the day we interviewed people one-to-one to get their impression of discussions so far. Several jurors told us that they had voted for 'restricting immigration' despite being afraid to raise it in the group discussions. As one put it: 'You see, even though no one dared to talk about immigration, they've all voted for it. It can't be ignored.'

In the end, more time was devoted to brokering a compromise on this one topic than any other. It seemed to be a shorthand for all the differences between the two groups' perspectives. Red Wallers pushed for a tougher limits on entry, judged exclusively by the contribution that can be made: 'Immigration is fine if everyone who comes in can contribute, but if I let in 300,000 and 100,000 don't have skills that we need, then they just become a drain on the system,' complained Angie from Bolton. Through discussion, however, we finally found some common ground. Everyone believed that the immigration system should be open and transparent with clear rules – rules that are fairer and more generous to people who meet the criteria. Everyone could also agree that there should be a clampdown on illegal immigration and that there should be an 'Australian-style' points-based system setting out clearly who should be allowed to enter. This was likely to be based predominately on having skills that the country needs. Urban Remainers were appeased by thinking that, once these grievances were addressed, immigrants would receive a warmer welcome: 'Stereotypes will change because we are letting the right people in...'

Finally, our citizens' jury set out to consider how these recommendations, initially positioned for an abstract ideal party, might land if applied to the Labour Party. There was clearly no point in developing a set of ideas that lost their traction when attached to the Labour brand. One thing that the two tribes could agree on easily was their fury with the Labour Party. Both groups were angry that Labour had not seemed serious about winning in 2019. They identified many flaws: persisting with Jeremy Corbyn even though he was known to be an unpopular leader; lack of party unity, a result of the poor leadership but also suggesting levels of incompetence that made it impossible to trust Labour in government. If that were not enough, they were also agreed about Labour's manifesto, its failure to set priorities or to provide a credible account of how its many promises would be paid for. Last but not least was criticism, again from both camps, of the 'fudge' on Brexit. This showcased weak leadership and, despite its apparent attempts to ride two horses, ended up pleasing no one. As one Urban Remainer put it: 'Honestly, Labour didn't even look as if they were trying. It just felt like giving up.'

The Red Wallers in Labour Together's citizens' jury, just like those I met through my Red Wall focus groups and interviews, although currently happy with the choice they made when they voted Tory, have not ruled out voting Labour in the future. But they have yet to be persuaded and need to be wooed. Meanwhile, Urban Remainers now want nothing more than for Labour to reinvent itself as a party that is actually electable. Based on the evidence of this citizens' jury, they are unlikely to go anywhere else in the near future and very clearly understand the importance of winning back disaffected voters – even those who disagree with them. Most would be willing to concede some ground to make this happen and understand the challenges ahead, hence their concessions on immigration. On the whole, they were much more comfortable with that compromise than the Red Wallers had been with giving up ending overseas aid. We closed the event by asking jurors to write postcards to the new leader. They came up with a raft of suggestions, mainly grouped into three areas. The first was to demonstrate strong and purposeful leadership. Here, they saw the main objective as winning back the disaffected and urged the party to select someone capable of doing that. The second was to show the party's priorities by identifying a smaller number of defining policies. And lastly, with the debate the group had just had on immigration front of mind, they urged the new leader not to shy away from or fudge difficult or challenging issues, but to tackle them head on with courage and clarity.

As I began my visits to Red Wall seats the Labour Party leadership contest was just getting underway. Very few people could name any of the candidates at first and it was pointless asking for views on specific individuals. Even in Darlington in mid-March I found that most people could still name no one, although there were a few mentions of 'the little blonde lass' and the 'lass with dark hair' and 'the dark-haired chap with a double-barrelled name' (who turned out to be the distinctly non-double-barrelled Keir Starmer). Instead, I asked them to tell me about the sort of qualities they felt Labour members should have in mind if they wanted to choose someone people like them might vote for. All the sessions identified several characteristics that might make them look again at Labour: being a strong leader, 'someone with a bit of backbone' who can resolve party tensions and reunite the party – without that there is little hope of persuading anyone that they can unite the country; being less 'extreme' was mentioned too: 'Fostering a bit of the middle ground would make whoever it is more appealing,' said one Red Waller. Given Johnson's great strength of charisma and 'X' factor star quality, several expected that a successful Labour leader would need to demonstrate a bit of this too: 'Whoever takes over is going to need to capture the public imagination,' explained one Red Waller. The most vital ingredient, though, is someone who 'gets me', and this is more true of the Red Wall voter than anyone else. 'Be for the working class,' said one. 'The working class like it used to be – people who actually want to work.'

I asked some of the people that I chatted to in Darlington, Hyndburn and Stoke for advice for Labour's new leader. 'Don't do it,' they joked in Darlington about what is dubbed 'the worst job in politics' in Westminster circles. For Kenneth in Oswaldtwistle, success comes back to integrity. He urged the new leader to 'listen to the public and understand what they want. If you can do what they've asked you to do then get on and do it. Do your best, do your very best. But if you think you can't then say you can't. Be honest.' In our online session conducted a couple of weeks after Keir Starmer's election, Justine in Stoke made the same point: 'Be transparent. Don't promise things you can't provide.' Colin, the brickie from Stoke, added, 'Don't forget about us up here in the north. Invest in the north

– it'll pay back.' If Labour were to follow this advice, could it win these voters back, I asked. The focus group of men in Accrington offered the most upbeat advice: 'We want to be given a bit of hope up here,' said one. 'Be positive about our future.' Another was even more prescriptive: 'Believe in this country. Just make this country great again. It's what we all want, and it's what Boris is saying he'll do, isn't it?'

16

CAN THE TORIES KEEP THEM?

'Why I voted Tory in a few words? They're not the Labour Party!
That was the main thing. The other lot weren't electable, to be
honest. But now I feel quite optimistic. Time will tell...'

In the summer of 2019, former Tory strategist James
Kanagasooriam began to 'play around with some numbers'
and noticed that if he modelled the projected Tory vote across
the country, he could identify massive clusters of under-
performance. In particular, he had spotted a stretch of seats
spanning from the Midlands up to the north and curling round
to North Wales, and another strip in the north-east. The Tories
had reached what he regarded as a critical mass of 30 per cent
of the vote in many of those constituencies and their vote share
had steadily increased by 15 per cent over ten years. He had a
theory about what was happening:

The entire area was slowly tipping and reverting to a mean.

It was to do with degradation of historical memory: Mrs Thatcher, heavy industry, coal mining. The economics that had driven those places to group together was being replaced by a cultural sense of belonging that was more proximate to the Conservatives.

As someone who had grown up near the coalmines in Kent, he felt he understood what was going on. He could see the potential for 'a complete shattering of Labour's heartlands'.

Meanwhile, in Bristol, psephologist Paula Surridge had also been crunching data. She reached a similar conclusion. She could see that, since 2010, some voters drawn from the 'traditional left' were beginning to look elsewhere. The crucial factor, she believed, was where those voters sat on a values spectrum from 'socially liberal' to 'socially authoritarian'. The further they were towards 'authoritarianism' on that axis, the more dangerous for the Labour vote. Labour, it seemed, just weren't on the same page on the things that these voters were most worried about. Some had become so disengaged throughout this period that they stopped voting altogether. Others began to flirt with UKIP. This disaffection became, as Surridge puts it, 'turbo-charged' in the Corbyn era. Combined with Brexit shining a light on the widening chasm between traditional Labour voters and the party, the potential grew for the eventual upset that happened in December 2019. Surridge's analysis shows that, in 2010, 12 per cent of 2005 Labour voters in Red Wall constituencies voted Tory. By 2015 this had crept up to 15 per cent, but then accelerated to 24 per cent in 2017 and finally, in 2019, a massive 34 per cent of 2005 Labour voters backed the Tories.

So, how easy will it be for the Conservatives to keep these new voters, given that two important obstacles to voting Labour (Brexit, and Corbyn) have now gone? Everywhere I went I asked this question. As we have seen, Boris Johnson succeeded in sweeping away some of the long-standing concern about the Tory brand last December. Although a lingering sadness at leaving Labour still remained, this was almost always about letting down older relatives, or a sense of being disloyal to the past, than anything currently salient to the voters themselves. Jean from Stoke was typical: 'I still feel really upset about not voting Labour – I feel I've betrayed my family, especially my dad.' Overwhelmingly, though, voters felt relief, and some even dared to feel more optimistic than they had for a while when they thought about the future. Ian, a plumber from Accrington, felt pretty good about his decision: 'The Tories seem modern – it makes me feel quite hopeful.' Most told me they were certainly open to voting Conservative again – even presumed it to be likely – but were keen to stress that this was not a foregone conclusion. Much would depend on what happened next. So far, most had concluded by early March, Johnson had made a good start, 'delivering' Brexit in the shape of the Withdrawal Bill, very much against the odds.

However, the delivery of Brexit alone will not be enough. In the pre-Covid phases of my interviews, I found that most were preoccupied by what they saw as the economic neglect of their place – in fact, most places in the north and Midlands

– contrasting with, as they saw it, the relative good fortune of London and the south. This was a resentment that had been building up for years. Expectations about what Johnson might now deliver were sky-high. No one, it turned out, had heard the expression 'levelling up'. Instead they envisaged regional redistribution, despite James Kanagasooriam's insistence that, as he put it, 'no one wants to someone else to be poorer so they can be richer'. He explained how he saw levelling up: 'It takes the redistribution elements of the centre-left mindset and allies it with a Thatcherite optimism of growing the economy … growing the pie, and sharing the pie better.' But Red Wallers believed it was a zero-sum game. Getting poorer so someone else could get richer was exactly what most suspected had been happening to them for decades. And they'd had enough. It seems the Tories too might face challenges in uniting the tribes that made up their voter coalition in December 2019. Paula Surridge's work analysing the British Election Study data examines the new working-class Tory voter. She explains that, while their most distinguishing feature is 'social authoritarianism', their values are rooted in patriotism and they are preoccupied with national security and crime. They also over-index on being economically left wing. Sharing the pie more fairly is exactly what's needed according to Red Wallers, and they see it as straightforward to achieve if the will is there. They imagine growing the pie, as Kanagasooriam interprets the Conservative aim, to be a far bigger stretch – especially in an economically shattered, post-Covid-19 economy.

Hyndburn was the first place I visited, in the middle of

February. Coronavirus was not mentioned once back then. I asked the focus groups to work in pairs coming up with three things that the Tories would need to do to keep their vote. 'Better infrastructure up here' came top of the list, exactly as new MP Sara Britcliffe had predicted it would. Andrew, a self-employed mechanic, worked through his arguments with Robin, a shopworker who had retired early for health reasons. 'Shift power north and end the north–south divide: make the Northern Powerhouse really happen; get all industries working together; bring investment back into this part of the world again,' summed up their pitch to the room. Everyone agreed: 'Spread the wealth across the country. I want to see some of it here, thank you very much. I'm being localist,' announced demolition manager Robert. Some of the older members of the group, like Gordon, were eager to see the return of old manufacturing industries. However, younger voters like Ian, a plumber, and Gary, a fitness instructor, had a different take: 'I can't see how manufacturing as it was can ever come back, to be honest,' Ian argued, 'But other things can replace it. Right now, there's nothing here at all. We need a flagship – something we're great at that can put us back on the map. We used to be the world leader in bricks and textiles here in Accy. Why can't we be the world leader in software or clean energy?'

My sessions in Darlington happened the week that would end in Britain's 'lockdown', but people had barely begun thinking about coronavirus. When charged with the same task as in Hyndburn a month before, voters echoed many of the same points, talking about 'getting our local economy into an upward spiral' again. Again, the north–south divide surfaced fast and the Darlington voters were blunt: 'We need more investment in the north compared to the south.' Some felt particularly aggrieved: 'We have less spent on us per person than they do in the south'. There was speculation that this was a legacy of the last Labour government: 'I heard that Blair did something to stop the north getting as much funding as the south – I heard it on Sky News. But they say Boris has torn it up to make sure that we get what's due.' Others thought that it was to do with favourable infrastructure deals designed solely to benefit the capital. 'They've spent more money on Crossrail than they ever have up here – and all it does is go from one side of London to the other,' complained Sue. All were agreed on one thing, however: HS2 is not the solution. Fundamentally, everyone believed that HS2's aim had been to enable spoilt Londoners to move around the country with greater ease. Several of the Red Wallers I met had never been to London, and those that had had typically only visited for an occasional family holiday to see the sights or take in a West End show. They had no problem at all with the speed with which they could currently get from where they lived to the capital.

Being unenthusiastic about the nation's capital did not prevent these voters from having the highest of expectations for what the new government might do for the nation as a whole. Almost everyone, in answering the 'how can the Tories keep your vote' question, reiterated the views expressed by the Red Wallers in the Labour Together citizens' jury, often literally using the same language: 'Make Britain Great Again'. Mindful of the contribution their place had historically made to the nation's wealth, this patriotism was intimately connected to local regeneration. Gordon talked about 'jobs and prosperity. That's how to make Britain great again: by doing trade deals across the world and getting people buying British. The way I see it is the sun never set on the British Empire and I'd love to see it all over again.' He clarified his point: 'Not conquering people I mean but, when they think about things they want, they come here – here to the UK – here to Accy!' What would they buy, I wondered. Without pausing for breath Gordon produced an impressive list: 'Medical research, financial services, aviation. A bridge from here to Ireland!' The room laughed with him, sharing his enthusiasm. He paused and shook his head. 'We'll see, we'll see…'

As we have heard, Red Wallers have little faith, based on their own experience, in the ability of politicians to change things. Back in early March 2020, Boris Johnson looked to them as though he could just be the exception that proves the rule and, on that basis, considerable faith had been placed in him. Although during the election campaign we found ambivalence, usually dividing along Leave/Remain voting patterns, most Red Wallers seemed willing, for the time being, to give him the benefit of the doubt. 'Give Boris a chance' was a sentiment that I heard expressed in those terms again and again. That said, we also know that Red Wallers, feeling detached from the centre, tend to place greater significance on local politics and politicians. Peter Gibson in Darlington had made an impact already, working with local hero and Tees Valley mayor Ben

Houchen. He had enjoyed early success lobbying for funds for Darlington station. In Stoke, Jo Gideon, new to the area, had had very little time to establish herself before lockdown began and was not yet achieving name recognition. She can, however, lay claim to achieving funds for the Royal Stoke Hospital, whose debt has been written off. Overall, Gareth Snell, former Labour MP, is optimistic for the party's future chances, but he told me: 'If I was the Tories, I'd put Royal Stoke funding on every leaflet between now and the next election.' In Hyndburn, Sara Britcliffe was already well known thanks to her year spent as a youthful lady mayoress. She also achieved some profile for her constituency by making history as the first MP to make her maiden speech online after Parliament was locked down due to the pandemic. She told me how determined she was to 'work hard, really hard' to make sure that Hyndburn benefited from the levelling-up agenda. The local authority matters too. All the new Tory MPs I met had benefited, to an extent, from the historically poor reputation of their local Labour council. Hyndburn's remains Labour, but Darlington and Stoke now have Tory councils, and expectations for them to make a positive impact on the local community are also high. And if they do not, the local MP will have nowhere to hide.

In BritainThinks' Mood of the Nation survey, the NHS was yet another thing for the public to feel gloomy about. We found that 46 per cent believed it would get significantly worse in the coming years. Unsurprising, then, that the NHS featured high on Red Wallers' wish-lists when they considered what would keep them voting Tory. Even pre-Covid, this was particularly true for women voters. 'We send the EU £350 million a week – let's fund our NHS instead,' the slogan on the campaign bus had screamed out. And, four years on, this hadn't been forgotten. Post-'Brexit Day' on 31 January 2020, the NHS had rapidly returned to the top of people's list of concerns, replacing Brexit, given that Brexit was apparently 'done'. Of course, many had their own tales to tell. Kenneth from Oswaldtwistle had had a near-death experience just two months before I met him. He'd been suddenly taken ill and, terrifyingly, the diagnosis was meningitis. 'They told my daughter I was a gonner. Told her to prepare for the worst. I was in hospital four week in the end. In the Blackburn Royal. But the treatment was good. Very good. I've honestly no complaint at all. And I'm here to tell the tale.' Just a week before lockdown in Britain, 58-year-old Bob was one of the few in Darlington to mention coronavirus. He told me: 'I'm a bit worried because I'll be categorised as high risk – I've had a heart attack – a serious one. I have breathing issues now because it was the artery that goes to my lung.' As if on cue he coughed and spluttered for a moment. When his coughing subsided, he gave me a wry smile: 'It's not coronavirus – we don't really have it round here. My cough is down to smoking – I'm still a smoker, though the doctors told me not to. The NHS were marvellous.'

The Conservative challenge is that, historically, the NHS has been a vote winner for Labour. Voters have tended to trust Labour to run the NHS more than they have trusted the Tories, so much so that the odd poll showing the Tories drawing level – as we saw occasionally in the run-up to the

2019 election – would make headline news. Even in the lowest ebb of the Corbyn era the NHS continued to be a unique area of strength for Labour. BritainThinks' leadership study in autumn 2019 gave Corbyn a small lead over Johnson for 'protecting Britain's public services for the long term'. Going into the 2019 election, where 60 per cent of voters, rising to 68 per cent of Labour voters, stated that healthcare and the NHS was their top priority when considering how to vote, Labour's lead was slightly reduced but still a comfortable 10 per cent. However, the party that founded the NHS back in 1948 cannot presume this advantage will last in perpetuity and there is a possible opportunity for the Conservatives here. I had been a little surprised by a vigorous debate that broke out in one Red Wall focus group because some were pretty certain that the NHS had been a post-war Tory Party creation: 'It was Winston Churchill, wasn't it?' Tracey had insisted.

The personal NHS stories I heard in the Red Wall were almost always ones of gratitude, despite the fact that all three of my chosen locations, along with many other Red Wall areas, fare significantly worse that the rest of the UK in terms of life expectancy, incidence of obesity, suicide and much more, according to Public Health England's published data. Many Red Wall seats would fall into the 'deprived areas' categories identified by Professor Michael Marmot when he revisited his 2010 review of public health for the Health Foundation ten years later in early 2020 – despite the then coalition government accepting all of his recommendations bar one. I was curious to explore recently announced government allocations to local authorities to cover extra expenditure necessitated by coronavirus. Again, I found that the allocations made to Red Wall areas were often below average, with Hyndburn particularly low. However, while Red Wallers were very fired up by economic inequalities, they did not seem to be particularly aware of the health inequalities that also often blight their towns.

Coronavirus may yet change that: certainly, by the time I spoke to voters in Stoke, we had all been in lockdown for a few weeks and the mood was very different. Of course, these Red Wallers shared the same aspirations for investment in and commitment to their area of those in Hyndburn and Darlington. They also shared the same loyalty to the socially authoritarian values that have so strongly favoured the Tories in the past. However, by mid-March the answer to the question 'Can the Tories keep these seats' already felt a bit different. While wider ambitions for their area had not been forgotten, for the time being at least the new government would be judged by its performance as it battled with what Boris Johnson described on his first press briefing after his own recovery as the 'silent mugger'. It was an interesting choice of words, and Red Wallers were now watching carefully to see if Covid-19 would rob them of the opportunity to correct those long-standing economic grievances. Even if the government comes out of the crisis with its reputation intact, if 'levelling up' does not happen in the way that Red Wallers expect it is far from clear whether the virus or the Tory government will be blamed.

17

THE ARRIVAL OF COVID-19

'I'm slightly optimistic that we may come out of this as better people, realising exactly what is important in life. This virus may turn out to be one of those rare things that changes everything for ever. So far, Boris has done a great job, I think ... but there's a long way to go yet.'

In *Talking to a Brick Wall*, I pointed out how very proud people were of the NHS, more British than a cup of tea, symbolising everything that is best about our country. As one focus group member back then put it: 'The NHS is fantastic – just brilliant – because it's fair and for everyone. If you get sick in America, they want a credit card just to say hello to you...' However, in 1997, after almost twenty years of Tory government cuts to all public services, many then believed that their much-loved institution was on its last legs, possibly so damaged that it had passed the point of no return. By the early 2000s the first challenge was to persuade voters that the NHS was worth saving at all. Labour advisors then went on to successfully make the case for a tax rise ring-fenced for the NHS. It turned out to be the most popular tax rise ever, approved by an astonishing eight out of ten of voters – including more than half of Tory voters. Labour's lead rose to 16 per cent in the aftermath of Gordon Brown's 2002 Budget setting this out, five years into the new Labour government and a year after its second election win. As discussed in Chapter 16, the NHS has remained a Labour strength even through the party's most challenging period.

Post-Brexit, the NHS had risen once again to the top of voters' priority league tables. Anticipating this, it was the other main focus in the Tories' campaigning activity in December 2019. That saliency now looks set to increase. As my Red Wall visits got underway the deadly coronavirus was tightening its grip on the nation. By May, the already embattled health service had coped better than expected with the virus but was struggling with the knock-on effect on its day-to-day service. Elective surgery had been cancelled, with operating theatres repurposed as ICUs, and thousands of retired healthcare professionals had been recalled for duty. Throughout all this the nation's affection and respect for the NHS and the people who work in it grew and grew. Who would ever have imagined that a regular Thursday evening routine for the British people would involve the very un-British practice of whole families standing on doorsteps, on balconies and at windows, clapping and cheering NHS staff. Every other house in my north London street displayed hand-painted posters of rainbows and hearts dedicated to the essential workers that the country was now so dependent on. It remains to be seen what long-term impact coronavirus will have on these views.

As Britain retreated indoors, BritainThinks began its 'Coronavirus Diaries' series, combining nationally representative polling with diary extracts drafted by fifty people from different walks of life all around the country, recording their experience of the nation in lockdown. We found their mood to be volatile. Initially it was characterised mainly by anxiety and fear as the seriousness of the situation hit home. These feelings then became tinged with sadness as stories about serious illness and death began to emerge. Although relatively few were directly affected, many knew of someone who had suffered from a bad bout and a handful knew someone who had lost a loved one. Although people told us that they were switching off from the news, the diaries themselves told a different story. In the election just three months before, Lord Ashcroft's polling had found that, typically, 40 per cent noticed 'nothing at all' each week. Now, our diarists were picking up extraordinary levels of detail on domestic and international developments and scientific and medical breakthroughs, all supported by stories of the impact on individuals. Captain Tom Moore, the 100-year-old veteran who became a national hero with his sponsored walk for the NHS, was just one of a number of news stories that resonated strongly with the public. The average person, watching three hours and forty minutes of TV a day, was increasingly rationing exposure to depressing news stories by 'windowing' current affairs viewing and watching much more light-hearted content. Viewing of comedy shows was up 40 per cent year on year.

As the weeks unfolded, we began to see frustration and boredom setting in. By week four, 'bored' was the word most often chosen to describe our diarists' response to lockdown. BritainThinks' polling found that as many as three out of ten now felt they were struggling to cope with the situation – rising to 42 per cent of 18–24s, who felt less worried by the health risk and more worried by the restriction. Some 34 per cent told us that working from home was damaging to their mental well-being. All this highlighted an emerging tension between feelings of fear and feelings of frustration, and 63 per cent were clear that, even if lockdown were lifted, they would still be 'too scared to go out'. An Ipsos MORI poll filled in further detail: it emerged that 67 per cent would be afraid of attending large music or sports events; 61 per cent of using public transport; 61 per cent of going to bars or restaurants; 48 per cent of sending their children back to school; and 43 per cent of going shopping. We knew that the government's 'Stay Home' message had worked, but now wondered, had it been too effective?

These anxieties dominated the narrative, but we also began to hear about the gradual awareness of the pandemic's economic implications. Although 73 per cent told us they were coping financially, many acknowledged that this was getting harder with every week and almost four in ten said that their income had already decreased. We heard some positive stories: office workers working from home on full pay were sometimes better off, spending less on travel, transport, entertainment and socialising. But generally the financial outlook was gloomy, with those with the most precarious incomes before the crisis hit hardest. Many told us that they would be taking a different approach to personal finances in the future, being more cautious on spending with greater focus on saving.

People were increasingly aware of the challenges faced by the government. The shortage of PPE for essential workers; the failure to meet targets on testing; and the growing scandal of deaths in care homes were suddenly never far from people's lips. Despite this, the government's ratings had risen to a peak net approval of 52 per cent by the end of March, the highest since the heady early days of the coalition government. From the outset, Red Wallers anticipated that Boris Johnson would take this in his stride, though an unexpected wobble came early when Johnson himself was struck down by the virus, then ten days later hospitalised, then, scarily, the next day taken into intensive care, apparently dangerously ill. This led to the first signs of criticism – albeit often somewhat reluctant given Johnson's situation and the abundant sympathy voters felt for him on a human level. Nonetheless, BritainThinks' polling found that 43 per cent were concerned that the government lacked leadership 'whilst Boris Johnson is out of action'. One diarist's feedback noted, 'The government is beginning to look a bit dishevelled – there is confusion at the top.' For the first time we began to see the government's soaring ratings stall. To add to the government's problems, the new Labour leader, Keir Starmer, was beginning to get noticed, and his call for a published 'exit strategy' was starting to bite, with 71 per cent agreeing that this was now necessary.

After a tough time in hospital – Johnson later described his situation as 'touch and go' – the Prime Minister recovered and returned to deliver a well-received and emotive speech praising the NHS, which he described as 'fuelled by love'. Following a further fortnight's convalescence, he reappeared to steady the ship. This was to be the peak of his own approval ratings, at least for the time being. Just a week later polling showed a 12 per cent drop in public approval of his handling of the crisis, albeit from a high 78 per cent to a still very positive 66 per cent. A positive outcome for the government suddenly looked less certain. I was reminded again of the reaction to Labour's performance in the financial crisis. Initially, Gordon Brown's ratings received a boost. However, this turned out to be temporary. In the short term the opposition supported his actions, but in the longer term they crafted an attack on Labour's fiscal responsibility that landed hard. It is also worth looking at the ups and downs of Tony Blair's ratings during his long premiership. It is clear that, at times of national crisis and collective endeavour, his ratings rose – the death of Princess Diana, the London bombings, winning the 2012 Olympics, all prompted spikes in his satisfaction polling – but these increases were never sustained. Gordon Brown, too, won his anticipated 'Brown bounce' in the first summer of his premiership as he grappled with foot-and-mouth, flooding and terrorism. But, similarly, this lead had faded away just weeks later.

Nonetheless, by May, the Tories still retained a comfortable poll lead: almost 20 per cent. It was proving difficult for the new leader of the Labour Party to establish himself with voters against the backdrop of lockdown. Starmer's room for manoeuvre was, in the early weeks, pretty limited. This didn't feel like the moment to attack the government's efforts but rather a moment for the political class to come together in the face of a common enemy. Sara Britcliffe, newly elected Conservative MP for Hyndburn, echoed this point, enthusiastically telling me that local organisations needed to become more joined up, and that she and the Labour council leader were now collaborating well together. She felt that this had the potential to change politics locally for the better: 'We used to each have a separate column in the local paper but in the past few weeks we've run it as a joint piece. Unity matters at a time like this,' she explained.

However, that unity would prove hard to maintain as the weeks unfolded. The government's first message – 'stay home, protect the NHS, save lives' – reflected the national mood well, and its simplicity and universal application made it hardhitting. By the middle of May, BritainThinks' Coronavirus Diaries suggested that cracks were beginning to show, with two camps emerging: one believing 'this can't go on much longer' and the other still keen on 'safety first'. It seemed that politics was returning too, with voters' reluctance to criticise the government giving way to a more febrile mood. As the government's 'stay home' message morphed into the more complicated 'stay alert', many voters' patience began to wear thin. Unity began to be sidelined as voter responses once again reflected old political battle lines: an SNP voter commented, 'Boris Johnson is a terrible leader, he has avoided any kind of accountability,' while a Tory die hard proclaimed his pride 'in

Boris for not bowing to media pressure'. Five weeks in, more people still approved (47 per cent) than disapproved (36 per cent) of the way that the government had handled the crisis so far. However, by mid-May new comparative international data became available suggesting that Britain may be performing less well than many other comparable countries, such as Spain, Italy, France, Germany, Sweden, China, Japan, South Korea and Australia. This news coincided with the PM's return to work and a growing list of missteps. BritainThinks' diarists started to talk about their 'shame' at Britain's relatively poor performance. The only country felt to fare worse than the UK was the USA: the country most often cited as home to the healthcare system that Brits most want to avoid. Patriotic Red Wallers would be likely to judge this reputational shortfall even more harshly.

It was increasingly clear that, whatever happened in the short term, the government's real test would be the longer-term impact of the crisis. Peter Kellner pondered this point on his excellent blog on 14 May, recalling the very different impacts that two political dramas in the past forty years had on public opinion. Will Covid-19 bring 'a new Falklands factor, or Iraq redivivus?', he asked. In 1982, on the eve of the invasion of the Falklands, just 36 per cent approved of Mrs Thatcher's performance as PM and only 32 per cent said they would vote Tory in an early election. By June, after the islands were recaptured, Thatcher's personal ratings had soared to 59 per cent and the Tory vote share was up at 48 per cent. However, the trajectory for the Iraq War was very different. Initially, Labour's and Blair's rating climbed a little, but as support for the war fell away, so did support for the government. Labour, while holding on in 2005, lost forty-seven seats: a similar loss would be enough to deny Johnson a majority at the next election, likely to take place in 2024. It seems that, while voters will rally round in a time of national emergency, their good will is not an inexhaustible commodity. Much will always depend on what happens after the crisis is over.

For this reason, politicians and public alike have an eye firmly on the future. By mid-May, many were already speculating that Covid-19 will change us for ever. James Kanagasooriam was convinced that this period would shape the future profoundly. When I asked him what the Conservatives needed to do to 'lock in' the vote, he answered honestly: 'Post-Covid, I just don't know what the answer is.' I asked, 'How much has Covid changed then?' He paused for effect: 'Everything! It's changed everything! It will lead to a rethink of how we structure the relationship between government and individuals and organisations. Rights and responsibilities will have to be more clearly delineated. It really will change everything.' Voters in Stoke, participating in our online focus group in April, agreed about the scale of the challenge and were worried that they, once again, might end up paying the price. Jean told me: 'We'll have to see how it pans out. But you have to reckon that the working class will suffer again. How are they going to rebuild the country?' Karen agreed, adding, 'Businesses will suffer, Stoke will suffer, the working class will suffer. Of course we will.' Justine felt that, post-Covid-19, 'a massive injection of funds' would be called for – it's only fair. I asked her what this would need to be spent on. She found it easier to talk about existing problems than to envisage new needs that might be created by the virus. 'We need something tangible. Regenerating Hanley properly, for example!'

The men in Stoke, weary of years of being let down by politicians, agreed with this but were also sympathetic to Kanagasooriam's point about how far-reaching the change that was needed might be. Always sharp-eyed on the look-out for politicians' sleights of hand, the Stoke voters could sense the potential to be 'had'. They felt that it would be vital to be transparent about troubled times ahead. 'Boris seems straightforward – seems to tell it like it is – but it's going to be hard,' pointed out Colin. 'The things we might have wanted before Covid-19 happened might not be possible now … investment up, taxes down, manufacturing back.' Pete agreed and wondered if they were starting to see the shape of things to come as they watched the government's crisis management: 'That PPE thing will come back to bite them if they don't get it sorted fast,' he commented. 'And all the data they're providing is rubbish. I don't trust that Matt Hancock either. He's made too many promises that he can't deliver.' Was the crisis starting to look, he wondered, a bit like 'normal politics'?

But even if some normality was returning to Westminster politics after Johnson's own recovery from the virus and return to the fray, out in the country it still all felt scarily different. Everyone was grappling to manage profound change in their lives. A small proportion had experienced personal tragedy and saving lives remained the top priority in all polling. However, by mid-May around a third – a steadily growing group – had also experienced significant financial hardship, and this looked set to get very much worse as most economists began to anticipate a recession that would cut deeper than any in recent memory. The implications of this would be far-reaching and likely to accelerate the transformation of Tory fiscal policy, potentially posing difficulties for both parties. For the first time since the election, it looked possible that Boris Johnson, even with his large Commons majority, may struggle to keep his own party behind what will inevitably be a sharp economic left turn. It also looked likely that Labour may continue to have difficulties differentiating themselves and making their case as the anti-austerity, pro-public services party against that backdrop.

Meanwhile, voters, more than anything else, were craving doing 'normal' things again, like hugging family and friends or going to the pub. However, just 9 per cent said they wanted us to truly 'go back to normal when all this is over'. BritainThinks' Coronavirus Diaries suggested that voters believed the country to be at a crossroads, with the potential to move in one of two directions: on the one hand, towards a country that is more unfair and more unequal, battling with deep recession, unemployment, public services and growing health and mental health problems; or, on the other hand, seizing the opportunity to 'reset', creating a fairer, more equal society. It goes without saying that the public were expecting – demanding even – that some good would come out of the grief. There was frequent and optimistic talk of the 'new normal', with 47 per cent believing that 'the country will change for the better in the long term', and, despite the backdrop of national division blighting Britain since the Brexit vote, 49 per cent thought that 'the crisis is bringing us together rather than highlighting divisions. As one BritainThinks diarist put it at the time: 'I'm slightly optimistic that we may come out of this as better people, realising exactly what is important in life.'

18

RED WALLERS VS THE 'ELITES'

'First with Brexit, and now in this last election, we've made our presence felt with the elites. I'm feeling optimistic but I honestly don't know what's going to happen next...'

In decades of listening to voters, trying to understand who they are, what they feel, what they need and what they want, I have never before encountered such a powerful collective sense of grievance. The voters that I met from Hyndburn, Darlington and Stoke-on-Trent felt neglected, taken for granted and patronised by politicians locally and nationally. The Red Wall seats are not a homogenous group in terms of their attitudes or their aspirations, but, while there are marked differences between the places that I visited, I heard the same negative themes over and over again. The deep sense of loss at the disappearance of their industrial inheritance; the abject failure to replace that lost heritage with anything that comes close to matching its glory days; the overall decline – decay even, in some places – of their local area; the lack of opportunity robbing young people of the future that they, of course, deserve. All had specific reasons to feel that their town had missed out, and that the north generally had been sacrificed to enrich the south. Thriving cities nearby failed to appease. Another unifying theme was the failure of the 'elites' to listen to and address these problems.

The EU referendum was the first moment for a long time when many voters felt that, at last, their views had been heard. The more that affluent southerners – especially Londoners – pleaded the case for Remain, the more entrenched many Red Wallers became in their choice to Leave. Fury at this being stalled was, for some, the first moment when they looked seriously at leaving Labour, but Brexit was a symptom not a cause of this disaffection. It had followed decades of growing disillusionment and decades of the Red Wallers believing they had been cheated out of what was due to them. Now, the most fervent hope emerging from the December 2019 election was the hope that they had, finally, been noticed, listened to and taken seriously.

However, both main parties, currently collectively owning some 80 per cent of the vote, face problems with Red Wall voters. Both struggle to look like the 'party for me' for Red Wallers. As we have seen, the Labour brand has changed dramatically, especially since 2017. Red Wallers feel they have little in common with the young, quinoa-eating, graduate, city-dwelling, socially liberal Remainers and Labour voters who, they believe, do not put Britain first and judge people like them harshly and unfairly for their views. Red Wallers also have little in common with typical Tory voters and, unchanged over the decades, the Tory brand is still seen as posh and uncaring, as superior as ever. Boris Johnson, with his support for Leave, his evident patriotism and his irrepressible positivity, successfully managed, by force of his own personality, to cut through some of these negatives. Ironically, his dishevelled appearance, a look so vilified in the early days of Jeremy Corbyn's leadership, lent him authenticity and, at first, he was given some benefit of the doubt. Labour also had an opportunity to make a fresh start as Keir Starmer took over as leader, but the Covid-19 crisis, initially at least, offered limited chance (partly due to the need to support the government effort and partly because of the restrictions placed on moving around the country) for him to establish himself much beyond the Westminster village.

Both parties have a struggle ahead to blend together a satisfactory coalition of Red Wall voters and their core vote. The old tribes have broken down, possibly for ever. While many loyal voters from both parties understand the electoral imperative of appealing to Red Wallers, actually doing so is unlikely to be a straightforward task. As we saw with the Labour Together citizens' jury, there are serious stumbling blocks ahead for Labour, specifically in the parts of the agenda described by Paula Surridge as 'social authoritarianism'. Views on immigration, benefits, crime, national security and even patriotism will prove hard to align without the kind of fudge that Red Wall voters sniff out a mile off and hold in contempt. The continued dominance of the Labour Party membership, so dramatically out of step with target voters, may yet prove to be an ongoing problem for Labour as it licks its wounds and tries to move forward. The Tories will probably find it relatively easier to unite around what many describe as 'socially conservative' values, but may encounter different problems given the Red Wall voters' passionate desire for economic redistribution and long held belief that they have been 'robbed'. Appeasing this is likely to clash with the fiscally conservative instincts of many traditional Tories. Achieving 'levelling up' through economic growth does not exactly hit the spot with Red Wallers, who believe the justice they crave can only come at a price, to be paid by those regions that have befitted in the past at the Red Wall's expense. But, setting that aside, even if it had looked like a viable strategy last December, the anticipated post-Covid recession clearly blocks that route, leaving the Tories facing some tough choices.

As I listened to Red Wall voters complaining about how politicians had let them down over the years, it was hard not to conclude that they were right – they had been let down. It seemed that depressingly little had changed since I wrote my book, *Talking to a Brick Wall*, ten years before. Back then I identified a phenomenon that I described as 'Peter Pan' politics. It wasn't just the Labour Party that had stopped listening to the voter; trust in all politics had broken down, in many cases deservedly. Too many politicians had played fast and loose with the goodwill of the electorate, and all politicians were now paying the price, forced to respond to voters' bitter disappointment. Then, it was about the financial crisis and the expenses scandal. Now, it is about the debacle of the Brexit process and may well, as the weeks unfold, also come to be about the response to Covid-19. However, I felt strongly then, and still believe now, that this problem is not just the responsibility of politicians. If democracy is to work then voters also have a crucial role to play, and, I would argue, a responsibility to play that role. This is surely as true for Red Wall voters as any other.

In 2010 I wrote:

Voters in focus groups have often admitted to me that they want to 'have their cake and eat it'. But voters are smart. They know that they cannot. Recent views on dealing with the deficit are a good example, where voters seek reward without sacrifice, yet know in their heart of hearts that this cannot be possible. They will punish any politician who speaks the truth, buy into promises that they suspect cannot be kept and then point the finger of blame when it all goes wrong.

'This,' I concluded,

is Peter Pan politics: politics where the electorate is encouraged to believe that they live in a version of never-never land, and is treated like a spoilt child by politicians desperately seeking their favour. Voters are offered gifts, made promises and sometimes lied to. Peter Pan politics means that politics is exclusively something that is done by politicians to voters...

Sadly, this is, if anything, even more resonant a theme in 2020 than it had been ten years earlier. In the conversations I had with

Red Wall voters, I heard about their genuine grievances. They really had been short-changed but, often, I found that they had taken very little responsibility themselves for engaging in the detail of difficult decisions that could have a profound impact on their own lives. Instead, they expected solutions to be delivered to them, with no costs attached or trade-offs explained. They knew there was a risk to this, and, frankly, often presumed the project would fail, preparing themselves to be furious when it did.

At the end of *Talking to a Brick Wall* I reconvened most of the individuals who had formed a voter panel in Harlow, a marginal seat I had followed throughout the 2010 election. We spent several hours together and, using a deliberative citizens' jury-style format, I asked them to develop proposals for reviving our democracy. Some of their ideas reviewed the role of politicians, including insisting that being an MP should be a full-time role, with MPs having stronger links to their constituencies, spending less time in London and more time locally, and that MPs should be more accountable, with proper job descriptions, training and performance reviews. Other ideas focused on voter engagement and included better political and economic education from an early age, better information on how policies affect you, published locally and nationally, more interaction between public and politicians and (good luck with this one) making politics 'sexy' and fashionable.

In some ways, a national crisis like Covid-19 forces the issue with some of these points. Government is no longer an abstract concept. Voters can see clearly and easily how policies and political decisions impact on their lives. They engage much more with current affairs, actually watching the news and reading the press and social media, and so are able to make a more informed decision about who they can and cannot trust. It is noteworthy that, so far, trust in social media looks like one of the biggest casualties of the pandemic, with voters disregarding information they read there much more than information they see on national news programmes. The most trusted source of information in the early days was the government's own daily press conference. Experts, too, much maligned after the Brexit vote, have enjoyed something of a renaissance in popularity. As we have seen, voters are looking for something positive to come from all the pain, and maybe, just maybe, one such positive outcome would be the chance to reset the relationship between voters and politicians to be more equal, inclusive and honest. It may be that this difficult time can offer a rare opportunity to change our politics for the better, and I'm certain that the appetite is there, especially with Red Wall voters who are just beginning to see the impact of the power they can wield.

After all the time I have spent in the Red Wall, I believe that, electorally, it remains firmly up for grabs. Though traditionally Labour, and despite more recent evangelism for the Conservatives, neither party is a natural ally for Red Wall voters. It will not be easy for Labour to win back, but nor is it a shoo-in for the Conservatives as they try to hang on to those seats. They will continue to have much to prove once the honeymoon is over – and even more after the Covid-19 crisis. Without doubt, this will be the battleground that determines the next election and, possibly, the elections that follow it, too.

With that in mind, as I have reflected on what I have heard from Red Wall voters in the past few months, I'd like to offer a few suggestions for any politician, whatever hue, who hopes to win the Red Wall vote in 2024.

1. Do not underestimate the extent to which Red Wall voters need to be wooed. Their tribal loyalty is a thing of the past. They now fully understand the value of their vote and they are determined to use that power so they can never be taken for granted again.

2. Wooing Red Wall voters means demonstrating how well you understand them. This will, of course, be easier for politicians who come from the Red Wall themselves and have a more instinctive grasp of their problems and priorities. While some local MPs fit this bill and cutting through at a local level will be crucially important, none of our current crop of national leaders do. Therefore, they must bridge the gap between their own experience and that of Red Wallers, whose values are rooted in their love of their country and their loyalty, through thick and thin, to their place. Red Wallers tend to have the closest of bonds with their family and their community. They work hard and resent those that don't. They are proud and resilient. They've had to be. Give them the respect they know they deserve.

3. Red Wallers are now demanding real, visible change and expect resources to be redistributed from the south to make this happen. They believe that people like them have been betrayed and that this must be corrected. There may

be a debate to be had amongst economists about whether the Red Wall's success must be contingent on this kind of redistribution, but my own sense is that Red Wallers will not believe any uplift in their fortunes is sustainable without it. They also believe, as we all do, that their children and grandchildren have the right to aspire to a successful future without moving away from their hometown.

4. Do not be tempted to soft soap Red Wallers. Their radar for noticing sleight of hand is very finely tuned. Building a relationship with them involves honesty and transparency, and, I believe, politicians will win rather than lose points by being true to themselves and by being truthful, even if the truth may not always be what Red Wallers want to hear. Again and again I heard Red Wallers talk up their own appetite for being consulted. Maybe the period of voter infantilisation and Peter Pan politics really is over. Try involving them. Try making them part of the solution. I really think they might just be up for it.

5. Lastly, but possibly most importantly, offer hope. Optimism, rather pessimism, has always been and will always be the hallmark of any election victory. Despite the scars they bear, Red Wallers want to believe that, at long last, this is their time. Realising this ambition was never going to be easy, and with coronavirus all bets are off, but Red Wallers have had too little to look forward to for far too long. They're hungry for change.

These five suggestions cannot be the end point. A truly happy ever after can only come from a relationship reset between voter and politician. And that must mean that voters take some share of the responsibility for making that relationship work better in the future. With that in mind, my final suggestions as I draw this section to a close are for the Red Wall voters themselves. I urge you all, ignored for so long and now realising your power for the first time, to use that power well. At the very, very least, turn up and vote. Voting matters and, while it might not always make as much difference as you'd like, it clearly carries more clout than not voting. And you can make voting work harder for you if you are willing to go further. Keep yourself informed so you can better call your representatives to account. Don't be fobbed off with false promises. Better still, get involved. You told me that you want politicians to be more like you. There's an obvious way to make that happen.

PART FOUR

POSTSCRIPT

19

THE CHANGING IMPACT OF COVID-19 AND OTHER UNFOLDING STORIES...

'Cummings is still there and BoJo is too frightened to dismiss him. At least, that is my take and that is the only explanation that makes any sense to me. We don't actually seem to have a government that can cope and respects us all enough to be truthful with us.'

My plan had been to close this book at the end of the previous chapter, but I had not anticipated the speed with which events would transform the political context and, with it, voter attitudes. In decades of observing and monitoring the national mood, I have never known it to be so volatile. The first few weeks of lockdown, culminating in Boris Johnson's own hospitalisation, saw the Prime Minister and his party's ratings soar. However, the 'Dominic Cummings affair', Boris Johnson's chief advisor's dash to Durham and subsequent day trip to Barnard Castle, marked a significant change in attitudes towards the government's handling of the Covid-19 crisis. The Westminster village and the media often get over-excited about news stories that, frankly, pass the ordinary voters by, but this one was different. Dominic Cummings has enjoyed fame that is rare for a government advisor. Back in February, 23 per cent had heard of him and 40 per cent knew who he was, making him considerably better known than most Cabinet ministers. An astonishing 3.7 million people chose to come inside on a gloriously sunny bank holiday Monday in May to watch him make a statement explaining his actions in a televised press conference in the No. 10 rose garden. The public was gripped, as if watching a soap opera, and, as they watched, the mood shifted. Almost every one of BritainThinks' diarists – fifty or so people drawn from all walks of life – mentioned him in their entries that weekend. Worried, even scared, at the outset, many diarists had grown bored as lockdown wore on and the grinding routine of their day-to-day lives began to grate. Now, for the first time, they were angry. The incident had ignited pent-up frustrations, simmering under the surface for weeks but now spilling over. Their fury was palpable.

Lockdown had produced a heightened sense of morality amongst the people I was listening to in focus groups and in those contributing to the diaries. What right and wrong looked like became an ongoing debate as people struggled to navigate this difficult time. Many reported that they felt judged by, and had also been actively judging, their neighbours and friends. BritainThinks' polling showed that 72 per cent believed they personally had 'followed the lockdown rules more closely than the average person'. Everyone had a tale to tell about someone they knew who had got it wrong. One diarist wrote about noticing that her next-door neighbour had invited family into her back garden before it was permissible to do so. She described becoming incandescent with rage, even though, as she watched from her bedroom window, she could see that those making up the small gathering were socially distancing and being careful about sharing food and crockery. She wrote that 'it took every ounce of my willpower' to not march straight round to their front door and complain. She had even briefly considered calling the police. Responding to these transgressions was particularly hard because everyone also had a tale to tell about self-sacrifice, hardship, even heartbreak. Lockdown had become an emotional roller coaster, with many feeling that their lives were out of control. Living on the edge, small things could trigger a meltdown. Another diarist wrote about having taken up knitting. Dropping a stitch in a scarf she was making reduced her to helpless sobbing that lasted all day. Against this febrile backdrop, Cummings's Durham trip – and Boris Johnson's apparently supine reaction to it – had acted like a lightning rod, fuelling indignation about people who don't or won't play by the rules. In polling a few days later, 70 per cent agreed 'there is one rule for them [the government] and one rule for everyone else': an unfortunate verdict on a government that had been voted in with such high expectations of ending that sense of 'them versus us' that was resented by so many voters, especially those in the Red Wall.

The government's ratings plummeted 20 per cent in two days – falling with a speed not witnessed since the Winter of Discontent in 1978–79. The Conservatives' lead in voting intention also fell by 15 per cent. Notably, that fall, although precipitated by Cummings's actions, had actually begun a couple of weeks before, on 10 May, when Boris Johnson made a TV address to the nation, changing the government advice from 'stay home' to 'stay alert'. The first, more sombre, message had been well received by an anxious nation eager to unite behind the government and support its efforts to beat the virus. Belying the warnings of behavioural experts, most people took the advice very seriously and complied. The more nuanced 'stay alert' message met a much less enthusiastic response. BritainThinks' diarists declared themselves to be both confused about what was being asked of them and worried about its implications. This worry was only compounded by ill-judged press briefings resulting in premature announcements of lockdown easing. 'Happy Monday!' the tabloids had screamed, promising the imminent opportunity to be reunited with family and friends. However, the polling was clear that, bored though people were, a majority still supported full-on lockdown and more than six out of ten said they would be too frightened to go out more, even if the law changed to allow them to do so. It seemed as if those first messages had, if anything, been too successful.

For the first time since the crisis began, voters started to seriously question the government's competency. Concerns about lack of PPE for NHS and care workers, and the release of thousands of vulnerable people still carrying the virus from hospitals back into care homes, began to translate into an increasingly grim death toll. By mid-June, an Opinium poll for *The Observer* found that just three out of ten now approved of the government's handling of the pandemic, contrasting with almost universal approval just a few short weeks before. One Conservative-voting, Leave-supporting diarist spoke for many with his damning diary entry: 'I think, at the beginning they [the government] seemed quite impressive and I had a fair amount of faith in them. Unfortunately, I now think they have made a huge number of errors. At the start I marked them five out of five – now I'm about to mark them zero.' There was growing unease that, despite the Prime Minister's boasts of Britain's 'world beating' response, the country was in reality faring poorly in comparison with other places. Now only 29 per cent agreed that Britain was doing well in contrast with other countries, while 47 per cent felt Britain was doing less well. Asked who might do a better job, half of the BritainThinks diarists heaped praise on New Zealand's Jacinda Ardern – someone many would probably have been unable to name just a few weeks before. A quarter praised Angela Merkel's leadership too, with some going on to comment on how well women leaders were doing at this time, suggesting the pandemic perhaps required a different style of leadership. As one diarist commented, 'This calls for non-macho, caring, humble, listening leaders. Women win while men continue to bluster … and I say that as a man,' he added.

Boris Johnson had passed what, for now at least, would turn out to be the peak of his popularity, reached at the time when he was in hospital battling with the coronavirus himself. His personal fight had been a vivid reminder of the viciousness of the virus. It had also been a symbol of the whole nation fighting this the disease together. However, by mid-May people were starting to question his leadership, and his personal ratings began to fall. Having at one time won over even his most vocal detractors, Johnson was now firmly back in the same place we had found him at the 2019 election. A divisive politician, loved by some but loathed by others. Both fan and foe agreed that his demeanour is 'bumbling' but, while some saw this as 'bumbling and inept', 'like Mr Bean. Super British but a bit strange. You feel maybe he doesn't completely know what he's doing,' others had a more affectionate and positive take: he is 'bumbling but brilliant', 'like Austin Powers. Clumsy, but very likeable and he might just pull it off.'

Johnson's likeability – coupled with his desire to be liked – was also proving a double-edged sword. Asked which animal he is most like, some chose a Labrador or golden retriever: 'He just wants to be loved.' A different problem was also starting to emerge for the increasingly beleaguered team at No. 10: some voters were now asking, 'Actually, where *is* Boris Johnson?' Of course, people had not expected to see him while he was ill, or even while he was convalescing, but now, although ostensibly back, his absence from centre stage at this crucial time was beginning to be noticed. Sympathetic diarists worried that he might still be unwell, while those less positively inclined began to speculate that he might really be as lazy as some had claimed in the past.

In week eleven of lockdown, BritainThinks gave the diarists a task. They were asked to imagine that a film was being produced depicting the UK's coronavirus response. Asked what genre it would be, dark comedy, satire or horror were the most common choices. Some diarists envisaged a documentary-style movie that was more supportive of the national effort. Possible slogans were: 'one country, one fight', 'hope was never lost' or 'we must never forget the strength of our nation when faced with adversity'. However, many more invented film titles with a negative take – sometimes using humour or satire to make their point: 'I'd call it *Coronavirus: A Farce*,' with the strapline, 'All there needed to be was clarity but the silence spoke louder'. Others revealed the nation's hubris: 'How about *The Shambolic Nation*, with the advertising slogan: "Want to see what happens when morons take over the greatest nation in the world?"' Many suggestions focused on the perceived shortcomings of the Prime Minister himself. One chose the title *Boris in Blunderland* for their movie. Another: *Where's Boris? – the Prime Minister deserts office in the midst of a global pandemic*,' or *Saving Private Boris*. We asked the diarists to consider what film critics would make of the saga. Again, the responses tended to reflect very negatively on both the government's reputation and that of the PM: 'I expect they'd give it a one-star review – it's too scary for the UK population to look back on,' commented one. 'A huge cast with very little action, depressing storyline and disastrous ending,' wrote another.

Meanwhile, opposition was back. Keir Starmer, elected as Labour leader in April, had initially struggled to make an impact, broadly supporting the government as the country rallied behind it, and offering what he described as 'constructive opposition'. However, as he did so, his personal ratings had continued to tick quietly upwards and, by mid-June, he had begun to draw level with Boris Johnson in the polls, despite more than a third still feeling that they did not know enough about him to offer a clear opinion. The early read of his ratings was that voters' views were divided broadly along party lines. In contrast with the PM's 'bumbling' image, first impressions of Starmer were characterised by 'intelligence', although this may not always be the compliment it seems at first sight. For some, it translates into wise and just: for this group, the fictional character Starmer most resembles is Clark Kent. 'Strong and sensible, there to do good,' said one voter. However, for others, exactly the same characteristics were driving suspicion: is he wily and sly, with a secret goal of undermining the government at this crucial time? Scar from *The Lion King* was the fictional character chosen by one. Overall, though, the polling suggested that the new opposition leader has made as good a start as he could have hoped for. An Ipsos MORI poll published on 12 June showed that 77 per cent of Labour voters were satisfied with his performance overall, bringing the party closer together than it had been for some time. However, more electorally significant was the fact that 51 per cent of all Britons approved of what he was doing, resulting in a net positive score of 31 per cent. This was equal to the best score achieved by Tony Blair in opposition and a better performance than that of the only other opposition leader in recent times to go on to become

Prime Minister: David Cameron, whose best ever score was a net positive of 23 per cent.

As the summer wore on and the mood grew even more febrile, Dominic Cummings's tour of the nation was not the only event to spark anger. On 25 May, George Floyd, a 46-year-old black man, was murdered in Minneapolis, USA, leading to world-wide protests about racial inequality. Campaigning group Black Lives Matter staged a series of marches and rallies all around the UK. The Bristol rally made headlines by culminating in the forceful removal of a statue of Edward Colston, a local historical figure who had donated much to the city but whose personal fortune had been amassed from slave trade spoils. After posting a carefully phrased 'I hear you' message in the black community newspaper *The Voice*, Johnson switched tack, apparently looking to get a rise out of Starmer and his team. He tweeted that to take down statues was to 'lie about our history', advising protesters to stay away from the second weekend of planned events and proclaiming how strongly he would defend Churchill's statue. Given the backdrop of 'socially conservative' past Labour voters choosing the Tories in December 2019, this was potentially treacherous territory for Labour. A few days later, another 'nod' to Red Wall voters was Johnson's announcement on 16 June that the Department for International Development was to be folded into the Foreign Office. Recalling that 'end overseas aid' was a top priority for Red Wall voters in the Labour Together citizens' jury, I wondered if this had the potential to kick off a damaging row. Certainly, Labour's previous leader would have actively engaged in the ensuing so-called 'culture war' that Johnson might have sought to activate and would probably have benefited from. However, Johnson appeared to have forgotten that he was no longer up against Jeremy Corbyn, and the contrast in style between Corbyn's leadership and Starmer's was about to become very clear.

It seemed that Starmer was willing to disappoint some Labour activists with a different approach. His response, voiced in the first of a series of live phone-in shows on radio station LBC, part of his *Call Keir* programme, was calm and measured. After being photographed alongside deputy Angela Rayner, taking the knee in his office as a mark of respect for George Floyd, he went on to criticise the behaviour of the Bristol crowd. He said that, although he felt that Colston's statue should have been removed years before, it was 'completely wrong' for it to come down in the way it had. In the Commons debate that followed later the same week, shadow Home Secretary Nick Thomas-Symonds echoed these thoughts, and also made a point of asking the Home Secretary, Priti Patel, about the welfare of police officers injured in the protests. This nuanced response seemed to accord with the national mood. In an Opinium poll published after Starmer's remarks, more than half of all UK adults said they also disapproved of the protestors pulling down Colston's statue, while 39 per cent also went on to say that they would have approved of its peaceful removal by the local authority. The following weekend, subsequent marches in London were marred by angry clashes, this time with far-right protestors, including one who was photographed urinating by the House of Commons memorial to PC Keith Palmer, who was murdered in a terrorist attack in 2017. The nation's heightened sense of morality was being tested as events took many twists and turns.

One question that BritainThinks has tracked regularly in its weekly diaries was designed to check whether diarists were more concerned about the health impact of the coronavirus or the economic impact. As time passed, most diarists held firm. Even twelve weeks in and after partial easing of the lockdown, health concerns continued to trump concerns about the economy. As the government began to try to coax the economy back to life, diarists still insisted that their greatest fear was not economic recession but a second wave of the virus. Responding to pressure from backbenchers, Boris Johnson announced a review of the two-metre social distancing rule in mid-June, but polling stubbornly confirmed that six out of ten would prefer it to remain the same and just 24 per cent would like to see it reduced to one metre. Health worries continued to dominate the diarists' entries, with many speculating about what they would and would not feel comfortable doing as lockdown became more relaxed. Polling showed that six out of ten would be happy to meet with family and friends out of doors, but far fewer were willing to interact indoors or meet with people they did not know, including visiting pubs or restaurants, browsing in shops when non-essential retail reopened or using public transport. This potentially hints at an emerging risk for the Conservatives, where the government could be seen to be at odds with voters, prioritising the economy over health and reverting to the perceived Tory norm of putting business first. This risk has accelerated amidst growing public concern that the government is no longer 'led by the science'. As I write in mid-June, voters have started to notice that scientists are now rare attendees at the government press briefings and speculate that this may signal their disagreement with government strategy – favouring the economy over health in a way that leads to measures that are not supported by the experts. It's one thing to question the government's competency in a crisis, but quite another to question its motivation, especially when the public are in the mood to judge people and organisations harshly.

Throughout the campaign, one organisation has thrived with an enhanced reputation: the NHS. As anxiety about health continued to dominate, so the nation's affection and respect grew, even though we no longer took to our doorsteps on a Thursday evening. As well as deepening affection and respect for front-line workers, the renaissance of reliance on experts continued with Chris Whitty, the chief medical officer. Whitty was rewarded with soaring personal ratings throughout the period, suggesting that he and those around him have the potential to wield immense power should the government and medical recommendations ever publicly part company. In terms of who is trusted to tell the truth about the pandemic, Opinium found that, while fewer than half trust the government as a source of accurate information (down from two out of three in mid-April), 90 per cent trust the NHS, 80 per cent trust scientists, doctors and experts, and 70 per cent trust global health organisations. Healthcare remains a rare area where Britons feel they can hold their heads up; they believe that Britain has fared better than other countries in managing this aspect of the crisis. However, there are now emerging concerns about the NHS's ability to resume normal service, and many claim they would still be too scared to visit their GP. Voters are clear about who is to blame for any shortcomings: the NHS 'have maintained a good level of care, but I would say with the closure of cancer treatments etc. the death toll will only get higher. This is not a dig at the nurses or doctors who have done all they can, but the government and hospital managers have been poor,' said one diarist. When asked what they would like to change after the pandemic has passed, better funding for the NHS and social care services is at the top of most lists: 87 per cent would like to see professionals in both sectors better rewarded – including those from overseas.

As the weeks unfolded it emerged that the government may well be facing a new challenge on Covid-19, specific to the Red Wall seats. Research published by the *Sunday Times* on 21 June revealed some uncomfortable data from forty-four of the constituencies. While the virus appeared to be receding in London, many of those seats in the north and the Midlands were showing a higher-than-average mortality rate. The overall death rate per 100,000 up to the end of May was 78.9 overall in England and Wales but in those forty-four seats was 87.7 – fourteen of which were recording more than 100 deaths per 100,000. While London's rate had dropped to 15.7 per 100,000, Blyth Valley, the totemic constituency that was the first Red Wall seat to fall, recorded more than three times as many. Penistone & Stocksbridge, another first-time Tory win, was the worst affected with a death rate of 129.5 per 100,000 since the start of the pandemic. That's eight times higher than London, which even at the peak of the virus had a lower death rate per capita. It is not clear why Covid-19 is hitting these areas so much harder. It may be an indicator of the wider deprivation that so many Red Wallers are bitterly aware of. It may be that many, as ex-mining communities, have a higher level of lung-related health problems. Either way, it seems to confirm Karen's point that 'businesses will suffer, Stoke will suffer, the working class will suffer. Of course we will. We always do.'

Red Wallers, and the wider public currently, have an almost impossible burden of things to worry about. Yet, it is perhaps surprising – and maybe concerning – that, as I write in June, the economy remains a relatively low priority. Although Ipsos MORI's issues index shows the economy rising up the agenda, with just 13 per cent naming it as their top issue in January up to 42 per cent in June, it is still a long way behind the coronavirus. While a third say that they are already worse off as a result of the pandemic, an Opinium poll for the Institute for the Future of Work in late May found that seven out of ten claimed to be as optimistic or even more optimistic about job prospects in their own sector as they had been a year ago. This is somewhat at odds with a People Management survey, which found that half of all employers expect redundancies in future months. While BritainThinks' diarists have talked about making modest changes to their own financial planning, it seems that few have any sense of the economic challenges the country is likely to face in the coming months. In early June, the OECD predicted a post-Covid slump in the UK's national income of 11.5 per cent, outstripping falls in France, Italy, Spain, Germany and the US, with a corresponding drop in employment. For now, voters seem to be continuing to trust the government on this: Chancellor Rishi Sunak is currently the politician attracting most praise for his handling of the crisis, with 60 per cent in June claiming that he has handled it very or fairly well (up 20 per cent since March). This gives him a net positive score of +46, comparing favourably with the government's overall score of -4. Monitoring Sunak's score in the coming months will be fascinating and revealing, not least because some are already sizing him up as a future Tory leader.

It seems a very long time since Brexit dominated the headlines – something that many members of the public make wry references to: one focus group member remarked, 'I'm fed up with seeing coronavirus on the TV, but at least it's not Brexit, Brexit, Brexit day in, day out.' It is, however, climbing slowly back up the issues of concern, landing in third place in June, 10 per cent behind the economy. YouGov polling in April, at the peak of the crisis, found stronger support for extending the transition period, with 56 per cent agreeing that this might be a good idea (78 per cent of Remainers and 37 per cent of Leavers). At this point in the pandemic, some queried whether Brexit should be a priority, claiming, 'The government has too much on its plate right now to handle the negotiations well.' Nonetheless, even at the height of the crisis, many Leave voters, and even some Remainers, strongly resisted any talk of delay, and instead urged the government to get on with it: 'We've taken years to get this far, let's just do it.' Attitudes towards Brexit may yet prove to be the one constant against a backdrop of tumultuous upheaval and change.

20

CONCLUSIONS: THE RED WALL RECKONING

'The government is a bit absent. They did such a great job at the start, but now lockdown is easing a bit I don't feel confident about what they're doing – I don't think anyone does.'

It seemed to me that the best way to bring this story to a close, for now at least, was to go back to where I had started, re-interviewing some of the people I had met just a few weeks before in Hyndburn, Darlington and Stoke to see how they had fared. I was keen to hear how they, and their friends and families, had been affected by the coronavirus: what had been the impact on their local area and had any of their opinions changed since we last spoke? I wondered, too, what they made of the new government after the dramatic events of the past few months, and how they felt the new opposition leader and his team were settling in. What, I wanted to ask, were their hopes and fears for the future and, crucially, what would determine their vote in four years' time?

I started by tracking down Michelle, the owner of an Accrington sandwich shop who I had last spoken to back in February. I found her packing her car up, ready to head over to visit her elderly dad in Cheshire. He had collapsed during the first week of lockdown and had been so ill that he had to be airlifted to hospital. Thankfully, he was OK now but, after a diagnosis of Parkinson's disease, Michelle was very, very worried about him – he was on his own and needed care. She was terrified when she thought about what the future might hold. I asked her how she was doing, and she sighed so deeply and paused for so long that I thought the phone line had been cut off. It had been an almost impossibly difficult time. She had had to shut up shop because, although she was a permitted trader as an essential service, she quickly found her customers had deserted her: 'There was absolutely nobody about. No one was going to work – there was no point in me being open.' Her supply chain had let her down, too. 'There was that shortage of flour. The bakery I use was a bit iffy about supplying me, because I was one of the little customers. They were baking but not the full amount.' I asked about how she was managing financially, and the question met another deep sigh. 'I spent hours looking into it and at first I thought I couldn't claim anything. I'm self-employed. I own my own property and I don't have a loan on the business. I don't have loads of children. After hours of research because I didn't fall into any of the categories, lots of studying, I thought maybe I could put in for something, so I did. But I haven't heard anything yet.'

Michelle had always been conscientious about her own paperwork despite the hours it took and now, at last, she hoped it might pay off. She had also found, somewhat to her surprise, that she was eligible for a grant from the council. This information came to her from an unlikely source, an interesting illustration of the country coming together in the face of the virus. She told me: 'I got two grand. The council didn't notify me, though. I found out from the guy in the corner shop – the foreign guy. This lot know every loophole that's going. I'd never have known about it if he hadn't tipped me off. He told me all sorts and was pretty helpful cos the council definitely didn't make it common knowledge. It was nice of him actually. He didn't have to tell me…'

It turned out that you had to have been trading for three years and be able to prove it. 'All your bookwork had to be A1 – no iffyness. The other butty shop down the road didn't qualify. It was a first – I never usually get anything at all but for once in my life I met the criteria'. It was a refreshing change from the usual injustices that Michelle had railed against when we last met: 'Accy is full of builders and roofers but they've not got the paperwork – often they're not even registered. Some of them are claiming benefits and running a bloody business at the same time. I've heard people complain and I've had to hold my tongue. It infuriates me when I think how much paperwork I've had to do over the years. I've had to have an accountant look it all over. It costs a lot of money and it's a lot of work. This job's not just standing behind the counter and giving people a butty, you know,' she explained. Now, living off her savings and the council grant, she hoped things would resolve quickly.

I had also been keen to talk again with Kenneth, the retired butcher from Accrington, but failed to reach him despite leaving several messages. I was worried as he had told me that he had been seriously ill with meningitis a few weeks before we met in February. I hope that he has been OK. I was relieved to catch up with Bob, the handyman from Darlington, too. He had felt himself to be very much at risk from Covid-19 when we chatted in March – he was a smoker and had had a heart attack a couple of years before. Thankfully, he had kept well throughout, he told me, sounding cheerful. He had stayed at home to begin with, but it had driven him 'crazy' and, after a couple of weeks off, he took a call from one of his clients – a school a few miles down the road that needed work preparing the school for reopening. He was very relieved to get back to work. He'd been busier than ever and happy being so. He'd felt a bit lonely, though, and told me how thrilled he had been to have an emotional reunion with his young grandchildren the weekend before: 'I'm welling up here just telling you about it.' Colin in Stoke and Ian in Accrington, also both in the building trade, had been working pretty much throughout lockdown, too. Ian, a plumber and handyman who worked mainly for a housing association, had been moved on to emergency repairs. Meanwhile Colin, who had himself contracted Covid-19 in the middle of April, a few weeks after we first spoke, had also kept going with his building work once he had recovered from what he described as a 'terrible time. I wouldn't wish it on my worst enemy. Never felt so ill in my life.' All three told me how grateful they were to be in work – they all had friends who had not been so lucky and had been hit hard financially.

Karen, the administrator at a school for kids with special needs in Stoke, also considered herself fortunate to have been working throughout. The pupils in her school, aged from three to nineteen, included some of the most vulnerable children in the local community, many with complex health and social issues. She estimated that the majority were on free school meals and described how, initially, the vouchers hadn't arrived and the ladies in the kitchen had been busy putting food packs together and personally delivering them to students' homes. Being there most days grounded her, she felt, giving her more of a sense of normality. That said, as the weeks wore on life was getting a bit monotonous: 'It's a bit like Groundhog Day,' she complained. 'I get up, go to work, come home, have dinner, go to bed, get up, go to work and so on and so on. Every day seems exactly the same as the one before.' When not at work, Karen had also been busy caring for her dad, who had recently suffered from throat cancer and was shielding after surgery and chemotherapy. Living independently, he needed help with shopping and medicines and she often dropped by to deliver to his doorstep on her way back from work.

How, I asked them all, did they feel the government had managed the crisis? The first reaction was often determinedly supportive. Yvonne Richardson, the activist who had fought so hard to save the impressive Darlington Library, declared that 'they had done as good a job as they could in very difficult circumstances'. Michelle knew one thing: 'I wouldn't want the job if you paid me, no way!' Colin believed that 'hindsight is a beautiful thing', telling me that it was so 'very easy to be wise after the event'. Many talked about the challenges of dealing with the unknown. Bob volunteered a score of six out of ten for the government and felt sure that 'anyone would have done what they did in the end'. However, as the discussions got underway, everyone I spoke to also admitted to some disappointment. The Dominic Cummings incident was mentioned by most. Yvonne was the most forgiving, firmly convinced that Cummings had only done what 'any one of us might do and put his child first'. She went on to berate the media and 'leftie campaigners' for hounding him when he returned home to London. Michelle had actually forgotten about the incident, although when I reminded her at the end of our chat it ignited her fury: 'I'd forgotten about that one actually, but it was disgusting. Disgusting! He should have gone – they think they're indispensable, don't they?'

The biggest fall-out from the Cummings affair was the impact on Boris Johnson himself, compounding other concerns as his authority was visibly shaken. Karen explained how she had been attracted to voting Conservative mainly because of what she saw as Boris Johnson's brave, bold leadership on Brexit: 'I voted Remain but quite honestly by the election I just wanted it to be over. I loved that he was very clear. Very firm and assertive. He's lost all that over this.' She had been sympathetic about the Cummings affair ('We're all human, aren't we?'), but now was able to list a litany of misdemeanours which she characterised as Johnson speaking out, 'speaking from his gut', then hearing more evidence and seeming to change his mind: 'Two metres! Face masks! Free school meals! We don't know where we are! He takes two steps forward then retracts as soon as he's challenged. We've got wishy washy back and I can't bear it!' Colin agreed: 'My opinion of him has definitely gone down. It's the way he comes across. Stumbles quite a bit. He needs to look like he's in charge, especially now. The country needs him to wrap his arms round it and take care of it.' Ian was downbeat too: 'It's obviously not been his finest hour. Some of his performances have been poor – waffle at a time when we need clarity. He needs to inspire confidence like he did in the run-up to the election. But,' Ian concluded, 'he was on surer ground then, and of course, he benefited from facing someone as useless as Jeremy Corbyn.'

The consensus was that Johnson was indeed up against someone very different now. Initial impressions of Keir Starmer were favourable, despite the fact that he is a sir, and therefore clearly, according to Karen, 'privileged and a Londoner', who, Ian felt, 'you could criticise in the same way as you'd criticise Boris. He obviously wouldn't know the price of a pint of milk.' On closer scrutiny, though, for now, Starmer's main advantage is quite simply not being Jeremy Corbyn. Even thinking about Corbyn got Michelle going again: 'I prefer [Starmer] to that pig-headed so and so. Oooh, I couldn't stand him, don't get me started!' The minority who watch PMQs felt it was telling that Starmer is 'a trained barrister', used to winning arguments, and that he did that well, emphasising Johnson's blustering manner while holding him to account. However, while several acknowledged the difficulties of the current situation – Michelle felt 'it was a tough time to start a job like that. Hard to get into the limelight' – most of the people I spoke to in June felt that, so far, they did not have a good enough sense of Starmer and what his Labour Party might look like to contemplate changing their vote, however disappointed they might currently be with the government's performance. Ian explained: 'He's patrician and very sure of himself – but hard to read. He seems to seek consensus, a middle ground, which is good, but in the end I don't know. I don't know what he's about. Meanwhile, I see Boris clearly – I get him. I genuinely believe that he's an old-fashioned patriot. He believes in Britain; he's not ashamed of the Empire. He's positive and optimistic. I think he'll stand up for our country and that's good enough for me.'

So, apart from the shift in party leader reputations, not yet significant to many Red Wallers, what else has changed? Everyone I spoke to told me how their life – and the lives of their immediate families – had been transformed. Bob's son had had to return from Italy where he was teaching, Michelle's stepson had been due to take GCSEs which had been cancelled. He had come back to live with her and was eating her out of house and home, adding to the pressure on finances: 'You've no idea how much a sixteen-year-old eats!' Karen felt so anxious that she was having vivid dreams and nightmares most nights. Colin's wife was recovering from cancer treatment and shielding, so he felt pretty worried about her. All had had to adapt unexpectedly and quickly and all were worried about what the future holds. Like the BritainThinks coronavirus diarists, they tended to be more worried about health than money – and also determined that health and care workers should be more appreciated and better rewarded in the future. They were increasingly worried about the economy, though, and several mentioned that they expected that their town would be hard hit: 'It usually is.' Colin felt that Stoke's shopping area, Hanley, had been 'a bit of a ghost town anyway – but now all the decent pubs and restaurants were closed and, he suspected, many were unlikely to reopen. He thought Debenham's would probably shut down too and feared what that might mean for local unemployment rates – bad now, due to get a whole lot worse.

That gloomy predictability of the Red Wall losing out was one thing that hadn't changed. Rishi Sunak came in for praise – the only government minister to emerge well from the crisis so far – but his furlough scheme, while generally well thought of, was also accused of being over generous with the cash of taxpayers like themselves. Bob and Colin both observed that the scheme was based, like everything else, on expectations of London and the south, not places like Darlington and Stoke. Bob told me that he had, at one period in his life, worked as a security guard for £2 an hour: 'I did it because I had to, to look after my family. And we were careful, we could live off that. Not a luxurious lifestyle but we got by. I don't see £2.5k [the maximum monthly amount that could be claimed from the scheme] as survival mode – it's a lot of money. It's the taxpayer funding quite lavish lifestyles.' Colin made a similar point: 'I think that two and a half grand is way too generous. Based on huge mortgages that people pay down south. Up here people live off a lot less – you can get a five-bedroomed detached house for less than £350,000 up here – it's a massive gap and another example of how we all fund the rest of the country.' Colin also suspected that the scheme was vulnerable to fraudulent claims. He knew people who were 'just enjoying ten weeks holiday courtesy of yours truly and who's ever going to know?'

Another constant seemed to be the reputations of the parties themselves. Keir Starmer's personal ratings may have drawn level, or even overtaken those of Boris Johnson, but, in June 2020, his party's reputation was failing to keep pace with its leader and still lagging well behind the Tories. This assessment was particularly true for Red Wall voters, tempted to the Tories for the first time in 2019 after the party had been 'de-snobbified' by Boris Johnson, at least for the time being. I asked those I re-interviewed what Labour would have to do to win back their vote. Even the minority actively looking at Labour again under Starmer's leadership were clear about the enormity of the challenge ahead. Having rejected the party at the 2019 election and made the break, several now felt that it would take a lot to encourage them to switch back. Pressing them to explain what they would need to see, the same five themes came up again and again. They are interrelated and, to succeed, Labour cannot treat the list like a pick 'n' mix. All the boxes must be ticked:

1. Establish Keir Starmer's leadership and set out clearly what he believes in. Bob's view was typical: 'Right now, I've not seen enough of Starmer to know where he will take his party. Not seen enough to really fill me with confidence. I want to know what he wants to do. I want to know what sort of man

he is underneath the smooth exterior.' Karen agreed, saying she liked what she'd seen so far but wanted Starmer to 'show us what he's passionate about'. Colin felt Starmer needs to 'pick his fights with care so we can see his priorities'.

2. Prove that Labour can be trusted with the economy. However well Starmer does personally, it will not be enough unless he can prove that he can take his party with him and address its greatest vulnerabilities. Colin was clear: 'My main worry with Labour is still the economy – can they manage it well, will they be responsible? It's especially important post-Covid-19 – it will be like recovering from a war.' Bob felt that it will be important to be reassured that Labour 'won't slosh our money around'. He was worried about taxation and felt the party needs to set clear spending boundaries and stick to them.

3. Get back in touch with ordinary working people. This comes back to the challenge posed in the Labour Together citizens' jury, which took place back in March. Can Labour retain its youthful, graduate city dwellers and also reconnect with working-class traditional voters? Yvonne in Darlington wasn't at all sure but felt it was vital that Labour listens more to people like her and stops assuming it always knows best. For many this means a new emphasis on the issues that matter most to them, like being tough on crime and reducing immigration. It also means demonstrating a real understanding of their aspirations.

4. Address the north–south divide. This was raised by almost everyone I spoke to and Covid has, if anything, heightened

the divide. Ian felt that, now more than ever, Labour needs to 'stop thinking that London is the be-all and end-all. We've got talent up here – use it – help us stand on our own two feet and the whole country will benefit.' Colin felt that 'Stoke's five little city centres will suffer the most as usual, with shops closing, unemployment and so on. Labour and Starmer need to get back into the northern heartlands and show us they know what's happening here and they care. They need to say, this is what we will do for you.'

5. Finally, Labour must set out its positive vision for Britain. Colin felt it could never be enough for the opposition to just criticise the government: 'They need to set out their alternative. Show us what they care about. Show us the Britain they want to see and the Britain they believe in.' A crucial part of this would be to counter long-held perceptions that Labour is not patriotic by showing that Labour really does care about Britain – and is as proud of it as Red Wallers are. As Ian said, 'I want to see them really stand up for the country. Show they believe our history is great, not evil.'

Meanwhile, the Tories, after a period of unprecedented popularity, seem to be enduring something of a wobble. There is now an aura of disappointment around Boris Johnson, who had given these Red Wall voters licence to dismiss their long-standing doubts about the Tories and vote for them, often for the first time. Most, for now, were inclined to stick with that choice, but were feeling increasingly concerned and starting to need significant reassurance. Again, Red Wallers had clear advice about what the Tories would need to do to keep their votes:

1. Stick to your Brexit promise was the first and most frequently heard piece of advice – even from Remain-voting Red Wallers. Ian insisted that this still mattered more than anything and that the past few months had changed nothing in his view: 'I've been anti-EU for ever,' he told me. 'It's already been delayed too long, and I'd be bitterly disappointed if it got delayed any more.' I asked if this would still be true if all that was on the table was no deal. 'Yes. Yes, definitely,' he replied. 'We just have to get on with it now and start making our own way in the world.'

2. Fund public services properly. If the economy is Labour's Achilles heel, proper funding of public services, especially the NHS, is a long-standing weakness for the Conservatives. Even in the worst doldrums of the Corbyn leadership, Labour was ahead on this. Now, Covid-19 has elevated the NHS right up to the top of many voters' priorities. Bob told me he felt that, while the NHS had managed well, the crisis had highlighted enduring problems that need to be addressed: 'I'm sure money has sometimes been wasted but things like the lack of PPE show that more money needs to be spent in some places too.'

3. Manage the economy fairly. Although for now fears about the economy are in second place to fears about health, it was still top of mind for many of the Red Wallers I spoke to in June – and likely to rise as the pandemic takes its toll. Many

were still concerned that a Conservative government would 'revert to form', placing the highest priority on big business and the wealthy. All were worried that it would be people like them who would pay the price rather than those more able to contribute. Bob felt sure that a tax hike was imminent ('However will we pay for all this otherwise?') and simply hoped that, for once, the Tories 'would do the right thing. I mean tax the right people – that is, the very well-off and successful businesses that can afford it more easily. It's always the little guy that takes the hit.'

4. Make good the investment promises in Red Wall towns. As soon as we started talking about the economy many automatically returned to this theme. Part of the appeal of the Conservatives in December was their pledge to invest in Red Wall areas. Few were aware of the 'levelling up' vocabulary (and probably didn't buy into the spirit of it either, being more likely, as we've seen, to believe that London and the south probably have to suffer before their area can thrive). But that agenda still matters and voters' appetite for it is undiminished by Covid-19. Colin from Stoke told me: 'Invest in Britain's future and when I say invest in Britain I mean invest round here – invest and innovate, otherwise where is the employment coming from? JCB are laying people off; bet365 may be in trouble if people are spending less. I get depressed talking to you!'

5. Strong leadership. More than anything else, when Red Wallers thought about how they would vote next time, all roads point back to one man. Boris Johnson had won them

over with his warmth, his authenticity, his patriotism and his clarity of purpose. Now, they were disappointed, and starting to wonder if he really was on their side after all. Karen sighed as she told me: 'People in charge have to have a grip on reality. They need to understand people who struggle. I thought he did but now I'm not sure.' Bob agreed: 'He's behaving like the upper-class Eton-educated man that he is – it all goes his way. He makes the rules, he breaks the rules.' Others were more sympathetic but still worried by Johnson's apparent loss of control of the agenda. Colin urged him: 'Be strong, man! Get a grip! Fight back a bit!'

There will never be a perfect time for a book about current political attitudes to draw to a close. Being in the middle of a deadly global pandemic, against the backdrop of a febrile national mood, with the worst recession the country has known hurtling towards us, a divisive exit from the EU still looking likely, and with a new Leader of the Opposition already showing potential to be a game-changer even before he's made his presence fully known, probably means now is the worst time. I had been ready to sign off a few weeks ago (around Chapter 18, to be precise) but that was before we witnessed, following the Dominic Cummings affair, an astonishing 20 per cent drop in government ratings overnight: the biggest and fastest fall witnessed since the 1970s. In years of monitoring public opinion, I have never known it to be so volatile. There are countless moving parts as we scan the horizon. I'm coming to terms with the likelihood that whatever I say right now may well turn out to be wrong – not just wrong in a few years or even months, but as soon as next week.

That said, some things never change. So much of what I heard when listening to people in the Red Wall seats in early 2020 chimed perfectly with what I had heard from voters all over the country in three decades of political research. In a fast-changing and sometimes scary world, voters, especially these Red Wall voters, continue to look for political leaders who combine understanding them and the problems they face, with the motivation and ability to do something about those problems. It has always been thus. And, for once, in a triumph of hope over experience, Red Wall voters are asking politicians to put them first. Both main parties have much to prove over the next few years.

ACKNOWLEDGEMENTS

Firstly, a huge thank you to all the people who shared their thoughts in my focus groups and interviews in Accrington, Darlington and Stoke. Everyone I met was kind, helpful, open and honest. I've changed their names here to protect their privacy but they'll recognise themselves. I hope I've represented their views accurately and fairly.

Thanks too to the politicians and experts I spoke to: Sara Britcliffe MP, Jenny Chapman, Peter Gibson MP, Jo Gideon MP, Graham Jones, James Kanagasooriam, Yvonne Richards, Gareth Snell and Paula Surridge.

I'm particularly grateful to everyone who read all or parts of the manuscript and offered such helpful feedback: Viki Cooke, Jerry Lockspeiser, Clara Pelly and Ben Shimshon. And to the brilliant team at BritainThinks, whose research over the past decade has given me a rich source of insight to draw upon. No one understands the national mood better.

The whole team at Biteback have been a pleasure to work

with: Olivia Beattie, Suzanne Sangster, Lucy Stewardson and James Stephens, as has Caroline Michel, my incredibly supportive agent.

Finally, and most of all, thanks to my husband, Dave, who kept me company on all the field trips, taking notes in focus groups (occasionally joining in the discussion before I could stop him), chatted through ideas, read and reviewed every word and made endless cups of coffee. I bet you're glad that I only seem to do this once every ten years…

INDEX

INDEX